# Communication Counts

# Communication Counts

## BUSINESS PRESENTATIONS FOR BUSY PEOPLE

**Mary Civiello**

with **Arlene Matthews**

WILEY

John Wiley & Sons, Inc.

Published by John Wiley & Sons, Inc., Hoboken, New Jersey.
Published simultaneously in Canada.

For general information on our other products and services or for technical
support, please contact our Customer Care Department within the United States at
(800) 762-2974, outside the United States at (317) 572-3993 or fax (317) 572-4002.

Wiley also publishes its books in a variety of electronic formats. Some content that
appears in print may not be available in electronic books. For more information
about Wiley products, visit our web site at www.wiley.com.

*Library of Congress Cataloging-in-Publication Data:*

Civiello, Mary, 1952–
    Communication counts : business presentations for busy people/Mary Civiello.
      p.  cm.
    Includes index.
    ISBN 978-0-470-17894-2 (pbk.)
      1. Business presentations.   I. Title.
  HF5718.22.C58 2008
  658.4'52—dc22

                                          2007050505

Printed in the United States of America
10  9  8  7  6  5  4  3  2  1

*Here's to my wonderful husband Bill.*
*He never liked public speaking but by seizing every*
*opportunity he now delivers the best toasts in town!*

# Contents

**Acknowledgments**                                                    ix

**Introduction:** Be Bright, Be Brief, Be Gone                         xi

### Part I: A Word in Edgewise

**Chapter 1**   Your Lips Are Moving . . . but Is Anyone
                Listening?                                              3

**Chapter 2**   Message in a Module                                    15

**Chapter 3**   The Fear Factor                                        25

### Part II: Message Boot Camp

**Chapter 4**   Audience: The "What's in it
                for Me?" Principle                                     39

**Chapter 5**   Substance: What's Your Headline?                       51

**Chapter 6**   Style: "V" Is for . . . Visual, Vocal, and Verbal      67

**Chapter 7**   Time Sense: The Lincoln Legacy                         87

### Part III: Presentation Situations

**Chapter 8**   Hold That Elevator:
                The One-Minute Message                                 103

**Chapter 9**    Meeting Modules: The Meeting
Meat without the Fat                          113

**Chapter 10**   Main Attraction Modules              121

**Chapter 11**   The Power to Cure PowerPoint and
Master Other Visual Aids                     131

**Chapter 12**   "That's a Good Question":  Handling Q&A   143

**Chapter 13**   Sharing the Stage:  Panels and Team
Presentations                                151

**Chapter 14**   A Moveable Feast: Presenting to
International Audiences                       161

**Part IV: Managing Your Media Moment**

**Chapter 15**   Reporters and Those They Report To    169

**Chapter 16**   Making Your Message the Story         177

**Chapter 17**   Serve It with Spice                   191

**Chapter 18**   Making the Most of Your Moment        201

**Part V: A Last Word**

**Chapter 19**   Oh No! Dealing with Worst-Case Scenarios   213

**About the Author**                                  **223**

**Index**                                             **225**

# Acknowledgments

I would like to thank many people for supporting me in getting this book written. First and foremost, my co-writer Arlene Matthews whose organization skills are surpassed only by her great sense of humor that I think comes through loud and clear in this text. I want to thank Marguerite Guglielmo, my manager, whose contributions are too many to count, as well as the team at eSlides in New York that created most of the illustrations in this book. They really know how to make PowerPoint slides tell a story and they can do it faster than anyone I know. I want to thank David Pugh and Kelly O'Connor at John Wiley & Sons for believing in me, and Judy Hansen for putting us all together. I also want to thank my friends and clients for providing me with great material that I believe everyone can profit from.

Finally, I want to thank you the reader for investing in what is increasingly prized: the ability to communicate well amidst all the clutter. Communication really does count, and taking it up a notch isn't tough if you make it a priority.

# Introduction

## BE BRIGHT, BE BRIEF, BE GONE

May I have your attention for a moment? No, really. May I have all of your attention, without your sneaking a peek at your BlackBerry or anticipating a cell phone vibration in your pocket? Can I have your undivided consideration—free from wandering thoughts about how to get the kids to their after-school activities or how much time you should really allow for getting to the airport—so that I can pitch an idea, ask for your support, or tell you a story that I hope will inspire you to change the way your do things?

Your attention is the one thing that anyone communicating with you must have if they want to achieve their goal. But let's face it. In most cases, you're not going to give it to them. Not unless they do a very, very good job of choosing the right message and presenting it: In just the right way in the right amount of time.

Now imagine the shoe is on the other foot. It's time for *you* to get a message across. Deep down you know everyone else is as busy and preoccupied as you are. Yet, if you are like most people, you have not adjusted your communication strategies to fit today's fast-paced, information-overloaded, attention-deficient world.

Recently I was working with a project manager at a startup company. She—let's call her Jennifer—had a lot riding on the success of an upcoming presentation, and just about everything working against her. Jennifer had arranged a meeting with several large companies to try to sell them new software. She had a great product that could save businesses a lot of money, but she faced several obstacles . . .

1. The audience: Any group she faced was likely to be skeptical, since her company's product involved a *new* application of technology.

2. The message: Jennifer was the kind of techie who didn't just want to tell you what something did, but also everything about how it did what it did. As a result, her content was cluttered.

3. The timing: Her meeting was taking place at the end of a three-day trade show. No one would want to do any heavy lifting. They'd want to go home—or out for a farewell cocktail.

4. Her style: Jennifer's response to short attention spans was to speed read—a sure way to meet a dead end.

Jennifer's problems were all common ones. Her presentation was simply too long and too boring—a potential yawn-fest at any time, and especially so when time was running out. But we were able to boil her pitch down to the basics and add a bit of entertainment, which put her project in the fast lane.

As you read this book you will learn what worked for Jennifer and what can work for you. Your approach to communicating will change for the better, and *you* will be better the next time you are up at bat.

*Communication Counts* was crafted as a quick and simple go-to manual for everyone who wants to communicate in a cacophonous, too-much-information world where it's nearly impossible to get a word in edgewise, let alone to have people remember it for more than a nanosecond!

As a former TV news reporter and morning anchor in New York City, the nation's largest market, I have applied television news know-how to help everyone from top CEOs to college applicants communicate better. Why do TV techniques translate to the real world? One reason is because reporters have always had a finite time to tell complex stories, and because they've always had to try to keep people from changing channels. They don't have to wonder if people have tuned out, they can get daily minute-to-minute reports showing when and how many viewers switched channels. In addition, TV techniques are perfect for business today because reporters know how to freshen a story for new and different audiences. At 11 P.M. no one wants to hear news they heard that morning. That doesn't work any more than a pitch to analysts works as a speech to your employees.

*Communication Counts* offers time-sensitive, flexible strategies for one-on-one communication, group presentations, and—because Andy Warhol's "15 minutes of fame" prophecy has come fully

true—media interviews. It also offers a unique or
approach that will enable you to say what you need to
that can best be heard and remembered, in a time frame tha
be flexed to suit any situation.

## The Modular Message

Today, each of us is required to be more verbal than ever before.
Television, the ubiquitous medium, has raised the bar to where
even the average person is expected to speak like a pro (even as TV
has, somewhat ironically, helped shorten our attention span for listening to that speech).

We must communicate our news effectively and efficiently if we
are to have a chance of being understood and well received. At-the-
ready communication skills are an essential part of success in virtually any business endeavor. Unless you're a lighthouse keeper or a
desert island landscaper, you'll get no free pass. (And won't these
loners be surprised when hordes of media descend for the next
*Survivor* series?)

If you want to deliver your news and capture people's stretched-
thin attention, you won't routinely find much useful training in
school or in the workplace. Yet, we are all expected to know what to
do and how to do it when we are asked to convey our ideas convinc-
ingly. Like it or not, we will be judged harshly if we come up short.

Enter what I call "modular" communications—the keys to your
communication success. Think of a modular sofa you rearrange to
fit an allotted space or to serve a certain practical function. Modular
communication strategies are like that: interchangeable, rearrange-
able, and expandable. They save you preparation time and add
power and resonance to your words. They are easy to learn and easy
to use. As Figure I.1 illustrates, you can arrange modular elements in
a linear format (see Figure I.a), store some modules away (see Figure
I.b), or even move and rearrange them around (see Figure I.c) as
needed to suit the varying needs of your audiences.

Got one minute to make an elevator pitch for a new account?
Two minutes to outline your business plan? Five minutes to convince
a headhunter why she should submit your resume for that dream
job? Twenty minutes to motivate new employees? As the various modular sofas illustrate, your message can be tailored for any occasion,
any audience. What's more, as situations change unexpectedly, you

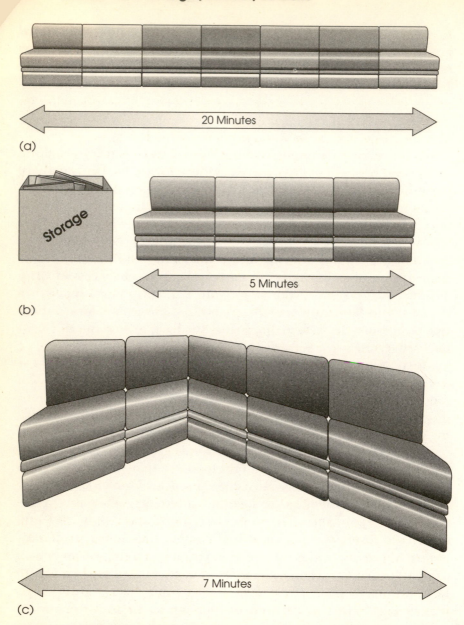

**Figure I    Message Modules Sofa: (a) Linear and All-Inclusive Arrangements or (b) Store 'em to Save Time or (c) Move 'em to Appeal to Your Audience**

can instantly adapt your modular message. If that proverbial elevator gets stuck between floors you will know just how to embellish your pitch. If you notice audience attention drifting three minutes into your 30-minute speech, you can shuffle your modules to lure listeners back in. That's because *Communication Counts* will help you develop your innate (but, until now, under-utilized) *time sense* along with *who, what,* and *how* communication essentials.

This user-oriented book is designed to help you cut through the clutter and bring your messages to the forefront when the stakes are high. It is based on the best presentation practices from my broad global client base and draws on the latest research from top business schools. It is written in a series of short, easily digestible chapters, which you may choose to read in linear fashion or dip into at any point for a quick tutorial or for a road map while writing your speech on a plane. And each chapter concludes with a brief "Top Tips" section to refresh your memory or to use as a cheat sheet.

*Part I: A Word in Edgewise* serves as an introduction and overview. It defines the key challenges facing anyone who needs to get his message across in a frenetic world. It introduces the concept of modular solutions and addresses right up front the anxieties that undermine so many potentially strong communicators.

*Part II: Message Boot Camp* delves more deeply into the concepts of audience, substance, style, and time sense, laying the groundwork for merging all these elements in a seamless delivery.

*Part III: Presentation Situations* walks you through preparation and delivery for a wide array of different speaking situations, from on-the-fly pitches to brief messaging in meetings, to lengthy presentations with or without PowerPoint, to team presentations, panel discussions, and more. For each situation, it shows how to think modularly about the four critical elements (audience, substance, style, and time constraints) and their connectors. It also shows how to think on your feet when situations change suddenly, when you're faced with a difficult question or a challenge from a listener, or when you're trying to get your message across in an international setting.

*Part IV: Managing Your Media Moment* is aimed at those of you who will be interacting with the media. Do not count yourself out no matter what your job, because these days this comprises a larger group than ever before. With a plethora of news networks and a host of niche print and online publications in need of 24/7 content, nearly everyone can—and probably should—avail themselves of the opportunity to get their message out via the media. Of course, media coverage is not always wanted, or indeed warranted, but that doesn't mean it won't occur. So this section also deals with making sure that challenging media moments are well managed.

*Part V: A Last Word* offers some final tips for worst-case scenarios, because sometimes life throws even the best of us a few curveballs.

When all's said and done, *Communication Counts* will have walked you through basic and advanced techniques for every verbal communication situation likely to arise. You will know how to cut through the clutter in a broad range of situations when saying it right, and in the right amount of time, will tip the scales in your favor.

# PART I

# A WORD IN EDGEWISE

# CHAPTER 1

# Your Lips Are Moving . . . but Is Anyone Listening?

How many times have you overheard a conversation in the hallway at work that sounds something like this:

**Employee A:** Hey, you look happy. What's up? Weren't you just in a meeting?

**Employee B:** Yes, I was in the COO's quarterly meeting on productivity.

**Employee A:** Well, did he have good news?

**Employee B:** No, not really.

**Employee A:** So productivity's not up?

**Employee B:** No, but I think he said he's got some plan.

**Employee A:** What kind of plan?

**Employee B:** Uh, can't remember. But I'm feeling good because while he was talking I finally went through my file folder and decided where we should go for Presidents' weekend.

We've all, no matter what our age, have the experience of picking up the phone to dial and forgetting whom we were about to call, of walking into a room and forgetting why we went there in the first place. *Who am I calling?* we ask ourselves. And: *Why am I in the kitchen?* In the brief moments it's taken us to begin an action, our short-term memory has been disrupted by countless, unrelated, fleeting thoughts. Let's face it: When it comes to remembering, we're not so hot. So why does it surprise most of us to learn that few people remember what we say almost as soon as we say it?

More important, what can we do to become more memorable? That's what this chapter will explore.

## The Forgetting Curve

The fact that most of us are not so good at retaining information is more than popular wisdom. It has long been backed by sound social science research. In the latter part of the nineteenth century, pioneering German psychologist Hermann Ebbinghaus—perhaps best known for his research on the learning curve—developed what he (somewhat depressingly, I think) termed the "forgetting curve."

The forgetting curve illustrates the decline of memory across the passage of time. And it's not a pretty picture.

Ebbinghaus' classic memory math tells us that people forget:

- 40 percent of what they hear by the end of a presentation.
- 60 percent by the end of the day.
- 90 percent by the end of the week.

This basic forgetting rate varies little among individuals, yet one fact remains constant: *Everyone* forgets.

This statement is as true today as it ever was, if not more so. A recent, often-quoted study found that the attention span of a contemporary audience starts to slip ever so slightly after—wait for it, wait for it—nine seconds.

### The Open and Close Effect

There is news you can use in that study: Audience interest is always high at the beginning of a talk, steadily slips, and then bounces back when the presenter lets on that they are about to close. Use that information to improve your presentations. Summarize periodically, and use other equally effective techniques that recapture attention through-out the presentation. I say jolt so they don't bolt, so their minds don't wander and they'll wonder what's coming next (see Figure 1.1). That is where my message modules will come in. You will learn *how* to jolt in Chapter 8, so stay tuned!

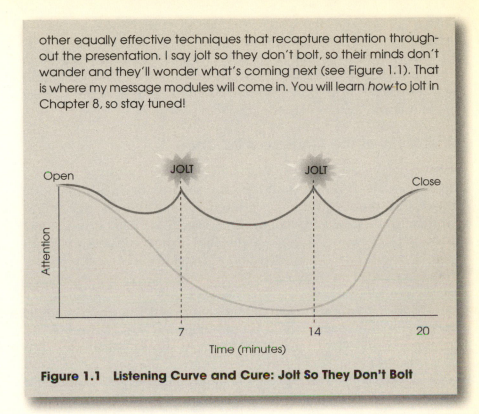

**Figure 1.1   Listening Curve and Cure: Jolt So They Don't Bolt**

## Did Someone Say Stress?

Another dynamic that Ebbinghaus noted was that people are apt to forget what they hear even more quickly when they are under stress. Now far be it from me to underplay the life stressors that existed back in the late nineteenth century. People back then worked hard and had families to care for, just as we do. They had far shorter life expectancies and, hey, they didn't even have the option of chilling out at night by channel surfing and snacking on microwave popcorn.

On the other hand, our contemporary environment is chock-full of memory-sapping stressors that no one back then could have imagined. The plethora of modern technologies apparently designed to enhance and simplify life has added a complexity component that is growing exponentially. Technology—everything from cell phones to laptop computers to PDAs—have compounded our conviction that we must maximize every moment, and meet, without exception, all others' expectations of us. Now, if you aren't available 24/7, you'll be asked why not.

So what's the result? If we are trying to *send* a message and present information we are faced with countless obstacles that prevent our words from being memorable. That is *if*—and this is a big *if*—those words even register in the first place.

## The Myth of the Captive Audience

Perhaps you are thinking that, at least in certain settings, you, as a speaker, will be exempt from the onerous memory math phenomenon. Can the forgetting curve apply to *your* listeners, you might wonder, when what you have to say is so critical? What if you're the boss or the keynote speaker or the highly paid consultant? Won't people automatically pay attention then? After all, there is something in it for them.

In a word: No.

Given the nature of the human brain and the many modern forces working against you, you should assume that there is no setting whatsoever where a speaker has a captive audience. Even if a group of employees, customers, board members, or industry analysts are obliged to be physically present for your talk, their minds can be—and usually are—elsewhere. How easy is it for people to pay attention when their cell phones are shimmying, their Blackberries are buzzing, and their laptops are merely snoozing—ready to reawaken with the gentle press of a finger?

If you want people to buy your product, buy into your plan, sign on your dotted line, or ask to learn more about your topic of interest, you'll need to learn to take memory math into account.

No, you can't change the human brain and you can't change the world, but you can change the way that you make business presentations so that your audience understands your message.

### The Crawl

Starting in the late 90s, many TV news shows instituted a permanent fixture known as "The Crawl," which is an endless text scroll of news bits that runs across the bottom of the screen.

Figure 1.2 is a montage illustrating the crawl on various news programs. Notice that news appears on the bottom of each television screen and can be distracting to viewers.

**Figure 1.2   The Mind Crawl**

As an exercise in reality checking, imagine your listeners' minds as "crawl-enhanced" television screens—with a constant stream of tempting distractions continually flowing by. Now remember: It's your mission—not theirs—to keep their focus on you. How are you going to do this?

## The Forgetting Curve's Silver Lining

So, now for the upside of the forgetting curve. (Yes, there is an upside.)

Retention rates can be increased in a number of ways. One is for listeners to actively work on honing their memory skills.

But because you have no control over whether your listeners will choose to devote time to mnemonic training (Nintendo DS Brain Age, anyone?) I won't dwell on that option here.

What I will dwell on is this: Research from Ebbinghaus' day onward shows that retention can be improved by packaging messages so that they are:

- Simpler
- Catchier
- More concrete
- More distinctive
- More emotionally salient
- More immediately relevant

Ebbinghaus showed that the forgetting curve is steepest for nonsensical material; conversely, people better remember vivid or traumatic material. Naturally I'm not going to suggest that you traumatize your audience (at least not if you can help it). But I am certainly going to suggest that you steer away from nonsense (an all-too-common currency in business-related speech) and instead say something different, say something differently, and make it say something to your audience.

Your first step on the journey toward memorability is to take an honest look at what may be some very poor communication habits so that you can uncover the essential elements of communicating in a memorable way.

## Essential Elements of Speaking

Memory math is daunting, but it's not the only thing working against us. The other memory-erasing element working against most of us is, well, us. We simply don't know how to say things in a memorable way because:

- We haven't taken the time to understand what motivates our audience.
- We are unclear about exactly what message we want to send.
- We fail to convey our message in a manner that makes an emotional connection.

Don't believe me? Consider the following real-life scenarios:

**Scenario 1:** Facing an auditorium of adolescents and their parents, the director of a prestigious summer academic program offers what he thinks are compelling reasons why teens would want to attend. For 45 minutes he elaborates on the inability of public schools to stimulate gifted kids and the frustrations of inventive students who are systematically bored. He lingers on his word-by-word recitation of PowerPoint bullet points, yet rushes through photos of what actually appear to be last year's program participants having fun. The parents look mildly interested. The kids, however—yes, the ones who are so easily bored—sport glazed facial expressions that imply recent mental departures to, say, the Andromeda Galaxy.

**Scenario 2:** A best-selling mystery writer gives a talk before her reading and book signing at an independent bookseller. The audience consists of devoted fans, all presumed book buyers. The half-hour prereading talk is about book tour experiences. The author's anecdotes are entertaining, but ultimately she communicates nothing except that she hates to do book tours but has to sell books. The potential book buyers can't help but feel a bit uncomfortable. Are they to infer they are putting the writer out? It's getting late. Should they stick around to buy a book or two as planned, or just call it a night?

**Scenario 3:** An executive at a big banking firm dislikes public speaking. He has his speeches written for him, then uses his prep time to nitpick the content, looking to add bigger, better numbers and changing words like "strong" to "robust." His staff dutifully takes notes but shares looks of dismay. They know he is purposely doing anything but what he should be doing . . . practicing his delivery. On an occasion where he will be addressing deep-pocketed potential clients, there is a bright spot in the script before him: an engaging story about how his firm helped grow one small business. But that story is the first thing the speaker cuts. In its place, he plugs in another graph he will describe in a monotone. Halfway through his talk, audience members begin to look longingly at their iPhones, their fingers twitching.

Each of these speakers has committed a cardinal sin of neglecting a communication basic. When communication counts, which is all of the time, speakers need to focus on four key elements:

1. **Audience:** Whom are you talking to? Whom are you trying to convince? What keeps them up at night? What do they already know, and what do they still need to learn?

    The director of the summer program failed to realize that if he wanted to persuade adolescents to do something, he needed to talk straight to those kids, citing things *they* cared about.

2. **Substance:** What, exactly, are you saying? Does your content support your message—or does it ignore or even undermine it?

    The touring author should have known that if she wanted people to buy her books, it wasn't smart to send a message that alienated fans.

3. **Style:** How are you saying what you say? Does your delivery reinforce and enhance your words? Are you colorful as well as clear? Are you perceived as enthusiastic, charismatic, and sincere? Is anyone getting excited?

    The corporate executive seemingly did everything in his power to take the vibrancy *out* of his speech. No matter how impressive the big numbers might be, they won't have the desired impact if they're camouflaged by flat recitation, rather than coupled with a story people can picture and thus remember.

    Finally, all of these speakers have ignored the fourth strategic element needed to get their messages across. It is the most important element in a crazy-busy world, where people are pulled in all directions by competing messages and where the nonstop background noise of technology and media drone endlessly.

4. **Time sense:** How long do you have to make your point? How long can you reasonably expect to hold people's attention given what you're up against?

    Both the summer program director and the novelist exceeded their audience's reasonable attention span. Kids weaned on *Sesame Street* jump cuts, video games, and text messages are a notoriously tough crowd. Then again, so are mystery fans that stole time from their already overscheduled lives for what they thought would be a relaxing break. These days, it turns out, everyone's a tough crowd.

As for the banking executive, he erred in the other direction. He could have held his initially eager audience longer if he'd served up his message with spice, and if he'd included the anecdote that explained what his company did for a small business along with an analogy that conveyed the idea, "If we can do this for them, think what we can do for you." He cut his presentation to shorten it, but he cut out the wrong material.

## Even the Best Can Blunder

You might think each of the people in my examples would have known better. After all, each of these speakers is bright and accomplished. What's more their various occupations *depend* on communication. But where, exactly, would they—or any of us—have learned the most effective presentation strategies for getting our messages heard? Even those who endured the obligatory public speaking class in high school or college could hardly have been prepped for today's information-saturated environment. We're not speaking in a classroom environment where certain standards of academic decorum (combined with a fear of angering the teacher) keep fellow students at least respectfully feigning attention. We are speaking in the equivalent of a three-ring circus—surrounded by competing attractions.

### Making the Grade

If the public speaking course you took in school wasn't the high point of your academic career, there is still hope for you. A transcript of Martin Luther King Jr.'s grades from Crozier Theological Seminary show his lowest grade was given in public speaking. He received a C.

In these last 7 years as a communications consultant and 20 years as a journalist, I have seen many brilliant speakers, but I've also seen virtually every communications misstep in the book made by people from all walks of life. I've noticed that our verbal communications landscape is populated with a lot of people who:

- Want to be quoted but are unwilling to say anything.
- Want to be controversial but are unprepared for a contentious reception.
- Fail to anticipate the obvious tough questions they will be asked.
- Fail to customize their presentation for *this* audience.
- Divulge too much, or too little, personal information.
- Ramble when time is short.
- Anxiously rush their messages when time is ample.
- Wander off message and never find their way home.
- Kill a momentous message with monotonous, redundant visuals.
- Choose jargon over genuine and memorable content.
- Fail to pinpoint the one key idea they want to leave with their listeners.
- Don't tell listeners what to do with the information they've given them.
- Appear completely unenthusiastic about their own message.

We've all witnessed how a communication snafu can derail a politician's campaign (think John Kerry's botched joke about working hard in school or "ending up in Iraq") or cast doubt on even an iconic megastar's judgment (think Tom Cruise's take on mental health as shared with *Today*'s Matt Lauer). But let's not cast the first stone. Sure, we've all been victims and innocent bystanders when it comes to communications debacles—but we've all been perpetrators, too.

## The Message Tripod

To remedy communications calamities, start visualizing any communication you plan to make as a tripod, atop of which a camera is perched. As you can see in Figure 1.3, the three legs of the tripod are Audience, Substance, and Style.

In photography, balancing the tripod is critical. If one leg is too short, your shot will be off or missed completely. Similarly, if you don't think about what your *audience* or listeners care about, what

**Figure 1.3    Tripod of Communication**

*substance* or message you most want to send them, and how to *style* or package that message, your communication will miss the mark.

But let's not forget about the "head" of your tripod. What's holding it all together is *time sense.* Every speaker should have a firm idea of what his audience's attention span would be under the best of circumstances. And they must know, as well, what to do when circumstances are less than optimal or when things take a sudden turn and they have to expand or, more likely, shorten their presentations.

In Part II of this book, Message Boot Camp, I'll look at the legs and seat of the communication tripod in detail. But before I do I want to introduce you to a very important concept that underlies Communication Counts: the idea of *modules.* Because modules provide the flexibility you will need to tailor a relevant, exciting message to any situation.

For now, remember this: You have to do more than move your lips to make an imprint upon someone's already overcommitted brain. Regardless of what you've learned, or failed to learn about communication in the past, you can avoid missteps from this day forward if you keep sight of *who, what,* and *how* communications basics while working hard to ensure you never, ever wear out your welcome.

## Top Tips

1. People forget over half of what they hear in a presentation by the end of the day, so make it memorable.
2. Summaries recapture attention so summarize periodically rather than just at the end.
3. To boost your message potency, think about the communications tripod: audience, substance, and style—as well as how much time you have to talk.

# 2

# Message in a Module

These days everyone needs to have a stump speech, a boilerplate that says what you do, why you do it, and why you do it better. It must be flexible, allowing you to shorten, lengthen, or shuffle it around depending on where you are, to whom you are talking, and how much time you have. Don't leave home without it. It is as essential to have on the tip of your tongue as any of the high-tech gadgets you want to have at your fingertips. But be prepared to do a bit of thinking before you "pack." You'll have to answer a series of questions, and once you do you'll be able to quickly prioritize and organize your message into movable, customizable blocks—those elements I call *message modules*. Remember, message modules are like modular pieces of furniture: the sofa with sections that can be quickly expanded when the in-laws arrive; the modular home entertainment unit with parts that can accommodate changing configurations of everything from giant plasma television screens to itty-bitty iPods. Wherever the modular units land, however, and whatever they hold, they appear exactly right—as if they were meant to be arranged exactly the way they are. As this chapter will show, modular messages serve the same function. They are portable units of essential information that can be tailored for a specific audience at a specific time, and every time tell a captivating story: your story.

## Simply Seven: Message Module Categories

There are seven types of message modules that appear on the modular message sofa. As you may notice in Figure 2.1, each of the types appears on a seat within the modular sofa. As discussed in the introduction, these modules are flexible, bendable, and moveable so that your message can be tailored to a specific audience while conveying a specific message. Moreover, you do not need to use all of the seven parts of the modular message sofa.

To begin, I'm going to give you a brief description of each of the seven modules:

1. **The Headline Module:** The headline module is the summary of your message. It is tellin 'em what you're gonna tell 'em. It encapsulates your most important point—the one thing you want them to remember if they remember nothing else. Your headline should be so portable that not only you, but also your listeners should be able to take it along everywhere. In other words, if one of your listeners is asked back at the water cooler what you spoke about during your presentation that morning, he should be able to repeat your headline more or less verbatim.

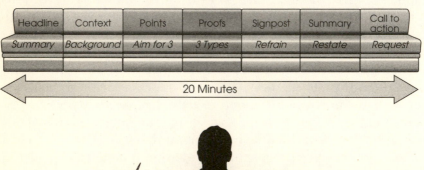

**Figure 2.1   Message Module Parts**

2. **The Context Module:** The context module provides background information needed to understand or appreciate your headline. Usually the context module is brief and has something to do with the past. It might be how the competitive landscape has changed; it might be an overview of what alternatives were available to you; or it could be a summary of what you've learned from past experience. The context module might also contain some of your personal or professional biography as it relates to your credibility. Note that context can be inserted at any point in your presentation as needed. It does not need to come at the beginning, although it might. You can also break up your context module and use it in different spots as needed to strengthen your points.

3. **The Points Module:** Points support and explain your headline. They are sub-headlines that offer depth and detail. You should try to develop three message points. More than that and people will be hard-pressed to remember them all. Fewer than three and they will sound skimpy. Think about it; good things so often come in threes:
   - Earth, wind, and fire.
   - Truth, justice, and the American way.
   - Liberty, equality, and fraternity.

4. **The Proofs Module:** Proofs back up your message points. They come in three main types: facts, analogies, and anecdotes.

   **Facts** can be financial or other metrics, accolades from a third party, an outside source, survey results, polling data, or outcomes of a study. Especially handy are facts that lend themselves to visual imagery, new and surprising data, or quotes from unexpected sources. Facts are absolutely necessary for credibility, but don't make the mistake of piling fact upon fact. Be sure to shuffle your facts with analogies and anecdotes.

   **Analogies** might make your blood run cold if you're mature enough to remember the old SATs (*kumquat* is to *fruit* as *lentil* is to *legume*). But what I mean is that you should create comparisons that relate your key points to similar scenarios outside of work. For example, you may want to compare your content to a sport, to well-known historical events or to familiar cultural concepts that everyone understands and accepts.

## Analogies Help Listeners "Get It"

Advertisers rely on analogies, too. Remember the ad where a little girl squeezed into a crowded elevator and then broke into a smile as she ran out of the elevator the instant the doors opened. The sponsor is Philips, maker of a new, expensive, open-bed MRI machine that they say beats slipping patients into enclosed imaging machines. Many people have not experienced MRIs and might not get the value, but the analogy in the ad says clearly: Closed areas = scary; Open areas = relaxed. To find an analogy ask, "What is this like?" Analogies prompt little "Aha" moments in which your listeners "get it."

**Anecdotes** are stories or concrete examples of your message points. Most of us remember a good story better than any other kind of content. If you think about it, the best teachers you had probably used stories to help bring subjects like history and science to life. We all remember what Paul Revere did on his ride and how Isaac Newton had his epiphany about gravity. We remember because we can picture these events, we may relate to them, and in doing so we can recall related facts and larger meanings. For every point you should think, "for example." Then try to tell your stories in three bullets within 30 seconds: set the stage, pinpoint the problem, and sell the solution. Provide a quick case study of who had a problem and how you solved it.

## The Three Amigos: A Mighty Trio

Remember the power of threes. Facts, analogies, and anecdotes should all be used to put meat on the bones of your three message points. Each should serve to reinforce and enhance one of your three proof points. The best-case scenario is to have at least one fact, one analogy, and one anecdote at the ready to back up each of your three key supporting points. Think $3 \times 3$—an exponentially mighty triad.

| Message Point 1 | Message Point 2 | Message Point 3 |
| --- | --- | --- |
| FACT | FACT | FACT |
| ANALOGY | ANALOGY | ANALOGY |
| ANECDOTE | ANECDOTE | ANECDOTE |

5. **The Signposts Module:** Signposts are short, catchy refrains that resonate in listeners' minds and that ring truer as you build your case. They are the hallmark of megasuccessful Evangelical preachers (Praise the Lord!), but they can be appropriated by anyone who wants his message to resonate. In business, you might use, "Profits equal promise." Who can forget lawyer Johnnie Cochran's signpost in the O.J. Simpson case, "If the glove doesn't fit, you must acquit!" One caveat: Use your signposts sparingly—perhaps three times: at the opening, in the middle, and at end. Signposts are like a potent spice. Don't overdo them (remember Al Gore and the "lockbox"?).

6. **The Summary Module:** In the summary module, you tell 'em what you've told 'em. You briefly sum up your message. Your summary should leave no doubt in your listeners' minds as to what you want their key takeaway to be.

7. **The Call to Action Module:** In the call to action module you tell your listeners what you want them to do with this information. Why are you speaking in the first place? Chances are it is because you want someone to do something: vote for you, hire you, work for you, work with you, buy what you're selling, believe what you're saying and get as excited about it as you are. But you'd be amazed how many times listeners leave a speech or presentation or meeting without knowing what it is the speaker wanted them to do. It might have *seemed* obvious to the speaker, but it was *not* obvious to the audience. Clear calls to action remedy this situation. They are compelling, energizing requests that you make of your listeners explaining what action they should be planning as they walk out the door.

## Connecting the Dots: A Case Study of Seven Simple Modules

After Steve Jobs, CEO of Apple Computer and Pixar Animation, gave a commencement address to the graduating class of Stanford University in 2005, his text was posted all over the Internet. Jobs was praised for his amazing, inspiring words. The speech, which came to be known as the "do what you love" speech, also happens to provide a useful demonstration of message modules.

In support of his main message Jobs used three key message points. He said that life makes sense in retrospect; he urged the graduates not to settle; and he reminded students to make the most of each day. Along the path of his speech, Jobs used a simple signpost, "do what you love," to reorient his audience. At the start of his talk, he tantalizingly promised his listeners "three stories." He alerted them when he was about to shift gears by saying, "My first story is about . . .," "My second story is about . . .," "My third story is about . . . ."

Jobs also gave multiple proofs for each message point. Weaving in personal anecdotes, he showed that life makes sense when you "connect the dots" in hindsight. He talked of his brief tenure as a college student, explaining that before he left Reed College he happened to take a course in calligraphy, even though "none of this had even a hope of any practical application in my life." But years later it turned out that what he'd learned directly impacted the design of the Mac as "the first computer with beautiful typography."

To underscore his point that no one should settle, Jobs gave some facts in the form of metrics, speaking about how he and Steve Wozniak started Apple when he was 20 and in 10 years grew it into a $2 billion company with more than 4,000 employees. Then he told another incredible anecdote about getting fired from the company he'd built, of being "freed . . . to enter one of the most creative periods of my life," and of coming back to lead Apple to even greater triumphs.

To prove his point about making every day count, Jobs told a story about death, or rather his near-miss with death after being diagnosed with pancreatic cancer (it turned out to be a rare, treatable form). He talked about how death gives life purpose and added that "Death is very likely the single best invention of Life." (That's quite an analogy!)

In summary, Jobs reminded his listeners to have the courage to follow their hearts and intuition. "They somehow already know what you truly want to become. Everything else is secondary," he said. And the call to action with which he left the graduates was short, sweet, and brilliant: "Stay young, stay foolish."

## Train Your Brain to Think in Modules

Now that you know what the seven modules are, you can easily begin to conceptualize what you will say in modular terms. Don't worry, there will be quite a few more pointers with regard to specifics as this book goes along. But it's not too soon to take a stab at it.

Here's how to go about beginning to identify and organize modules:

**Take an inventory:** The first thing you can do is to look over any speech or presentation content you have already created. Can you find your headline and message points? Do you notice any proofs in the form of facts, analogies, or anecdotes? Label these items as such. Likewise, label any signposts—or something you believe has the potential to be a signpost—as well as contextual statements and calls to action.

**Notice any gaps:** If you're like most people you'll notice that there are some missing elements in your content. Don't worry about them for now, but do make a note of them. What do you need? Analogies? A signpost? Some relevant historical or biographical framing? Note, too, what content you already have that could do with some improvement. Is your call to action compelling enough? Is it specific enough? Is your headline clear enough? Be your own critic so that your audience will not have to criticize.

**Create new content:** Now that you know what you need, ideas will probably start popping up everywhere. I call this the "You See What You Look For" phenomenon. Think about what it is you most want to say and then remain on the alert for anything and everything that reinforces your message. Skim newspapers and magazines for current stories that offer relevant facts or context. Make a note whenever you see a similar situation arise (raw material for your analogies). Examine your daily life for anecdotes that provide a human touch. You will be amazed how the elements you require to build your modules just seem to show up once your radar becomes activated.

**Keep track:** Devise a simple system for classifying and organizing the modules you've identified. You can do this electronically by creating files and folders on your computer. In Figure 2.2, I have provided an illustration of how you can use your computer to keep track of your modules. First, start by creating seven file folders and label them with each modular message name (see Figure 2.2a). Then, for example, when you hear a poignant line or story, file the information in the "Signposts" folder (see Figure 2.2b); or when you see facts

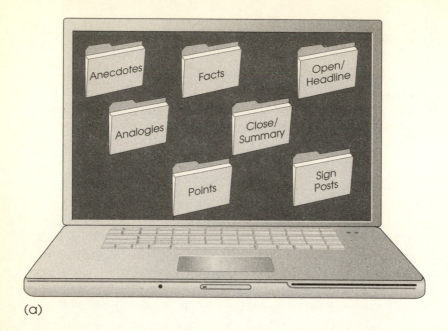

(a)

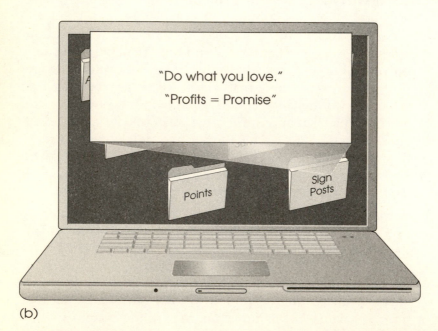

(b)

**Figure 2.2    Filing Away Your Modules: (a) File Your Message Modules; (b) File Away Your Signposts; (c) File Your Facts; (d) File Your Analogies**

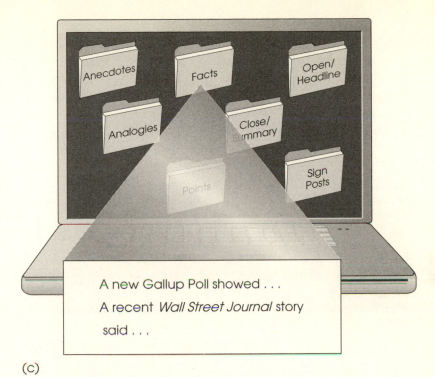

(c)

An MRI feels like being in an elevator that stalls at lunchtime. You're squeezed in, it's scary. Our system feels like when the elevator doors open!

I saw an ad the other day that says it all . . .

(d)

**Figure 2.2**    *(Continued)*

in a newspaper or journal article, file them in the "Facts" folder (see Figure 2.2c); or when you see an ad that relates to the subject matter you will be presenting during one of your business presentations, I file it in the "Analogies" folder (see Figure 2.2d). I find this much better than my old method of filing newspaper clippings in the bottom of my purse. That was good only for used gum.

If you prefer low-tech, try using index cards or a notepad on which you can jot ideas as they occur to you. You might even use different color cards to denote different modules. This method allows you to literally shuffle modules around to try out different orders or to edit a long message down to a shorter one in a flash. You should use whatever works for you.

**Experiment:** Modular messages are, by design, infinitely adaptable. Don't be afraid to experiment. Try your messages in various lengths, add an anecdote or analogy and see how it impacts the flow. Most important of all, don't freeze your modules. Remain open to new content that will make your message more potent; delete things that don't seem to be working, that bog you down, or that do not seem as clear as they could be.

In the remainder of this book, I'll help you refine the elements of your message further. But before I do so, it's time to address something that I suspect is nagging at many of you. "It's all very well to have my modules," you might be thinking, "but they won't help me with my anxiety about speaking in public."

Or will they?

## Top Tips

1. Aim for just three points regardless of how long your presentation is. More than that will be forgotten.
2. Keep message module folders on your computer and refresh whenever you see or hear news you can use in your next presentation.
3. Don't forget the Call to Action in your presentations. You know the advice: Tell 'em what you'll tell 'em, tell 'em, and tell 'em what you told 'em. Then, tell 'em what you want them to do with it!

# CHAPTER 3

# The Fear Factor

What are you most afraid of? Heights? Flying? Killer bees? For most people, public speaking tops the list—trumping even the fear of dying. That prompted Jerry Seinfeld to quip that if people fear speaking more than death, at a funeral they'd rather be lying in the coffin than delivering the eulogy.

If you're scared stiff about standing up and speaking in front of a group, you're not alone. Some of our greatest orators have felt the same way. The young Mahatma Gandhi, working as a lawyer, actually fainted from anxiety the first time he had to present a case in court. So that's the good news: In your misery you have lots of excellent company.

The bad news is that in today's business environment, no one is going to cut you any slack because you don't like to talk in front of a group of people. Ever since the advent of PowerPoint, everyone seems to be expected to "just do it," which is a little odd when you think about it, as if the invention of state-of-the-art deep sea diving equipment meant everyone should suddenly feel comfortable plunging into the ocean's depths. But try complaining to your boss that you just aren't comfortable with public speaking, and you are not apt to get much sympathy, let alone fewer such assignments. And, no, even the Mahatma Gandhi anecdote will not get you off the hook. There's work to be done, information to be imparted. You can't wimp out.

But don't despair. This chapter is here to help and the first step is to think about what your fear really consists of.

### Tongue-Tied?

The fear of public speaking is believed to be the most common phobia, affecting some 75 percent of the population. Stage fright is bipartisan. George McGovern suffered stage fright. And, according to speechwriter Peggy Noonan, even Ronald Reagan, the so-called "great communicator," was nervous before every speech.

By the way, even being spectacularly bad at public speaking won't relieve you of such duties, so don't make the mistake of thinking that giving one alarmingly dull presentation will get you taken out of the presentation rotation. Your audience may be dazed instead of dazzled, but they won't banish you from the podium—especially if it means that *they* would have to do more speaking. Chances are they don't like doing it any more than you do.

The reality is that there is no way around the fear of public speaking; you simply must go through it.

## Yikes! The Physical Aspect of Speaker's Fear

You may have heard or read in many places, as I have, that stressful situations, that is, situations where we react to a perceived threat like the presence of a man-eating tiger, instigate our body's fight or flight response. The part of our autonomic nervous system that is wired to protect and defend us from danger accelerates our heart rate, quickens our breath, and diverts blood to our muscles (the better to run away from the tiger). It dilates our pupils (the better to see our bloodthirsty attacker) and dries out our mouth (this is no time to have a sandwich—unless you want to end up a sandwich!). Our body temperature alters, too, and as a result our hands get cold and clammy; our foreheads get sweaty.

Although speaking in public surely does not present the same magnitude of threat as facing down carnivorous predators, your body can't really tell the difference. If you interpret the situation as a threat, your nervous system will respond with the fight or flight response. Tens of thousands of years of evolution have made it so.

But fight or flight, as you have doubtless already figured out, represents a somewhat limited range of options when it comes to delivering business presentations. After all, there's no one to fight; you're supposed to woo the audience, not punch them out. And there's nowhere to run; sure you can duck into the restroom for two minutes, but sooner or later you've got to come out and face your boss and colleagues or audience.

The standard advice with regard to managing the physical aspects of fear or stress is roughly akin to that of making lemonade from lemons—taking a negative and turning it into a positive. If you make it a point to cognitively reinterpret your physical symptoms as energy providing power jolts, you can reframe your anxiety as a source of performance strength. This is not bad advice, in fact, it is sound, as far as delivering presentations goes. People who actually enjoy speaking and presenting do indeed use their jitters, rather than succumbing to them, trying to ignore them, or wishing they would go away. They feel the butterflies in their stomachs and instead of thinking, "Oh, no, not this again," they think, "Ah, right on schedule. I'm ready." As Helen Hayes, the renowned "first lady of theater," put it: "I still get butterflies before every performance. But over the years I've managed to teach them to fly in formation."

Contrary to what you might imagine, it would not be best to banish the butterflies altogether—even if you could. Studies confirm that all kinds of professional performers, from stand-up comics to pro golfers to concert violinists, do better if they have a moderate degree of preperformance nerves. Note that the key word here is *moderate*. Before you can reframe your fear as energizing rather than excruciating, you need to move it off its highest setting, that is, turn down its volume a bit. That involves looking at the little subworries that feed your overall anxious state.

## Keep Your Butterflies in Your Own Net

The one thing you do *not* want to do is to get up and tell everyone that you are nervous. Saying so won't make you any less so, and it will make the audience look for signs of trouble instead of listening to what you have to say.

## What Will They Think of Me? The Cognitive Aspect of Speaker's Fear

In my years spent training high-powered executives and celebrities—hardly nervous or self-effacing types in most situations—I've learned that often it's not actually the fear of talking in front of people *per se* that is so daunting. When you dig deeper, you find out that what really makes many of us fearful of public discourse are concerns about other people's perceptions of us such as:

- I won't be perceived as the sharpest pencil in the box.
- I won't be believable.
- I won't be likeable.
- Something will go wrong; I'll be—literally—speechless, and come off as inept.

Creating modular messages can actually help you cope with each of these concerns. You are no doubt familiar with the Boy Scout motto: Be prepared. With modules in your pocket, so to speak, you will be prepared for anything, and thus be perceived as smart, believable, likeable, and strong.

### The Sharp Pencil Makes a Point

One cognitive aspect of speakers' fears is that they worry that they will not be perceived as the sharpest pencil in the box or the brightest bulb in the batch. However, people should not fear that they will come across as unintelligent. After all, when people gather to hear a presentation they hope for a few basic things. The most basic thing they want is information. The things they don't want are boredom, confusion, or bull. Anything they get on top of an engagingly presented, well-organized and informative presentation—such as entertainment, humor, inspiration, motivation, revelation—is icing on the cake. If you want to speak intelligently and present the information in an organized, audience-friendly fashion, start with the basics. Use your headline module to make sure that everyone knows the theme of your presentation. Imagine your audience seeing your headline splayed across the front page of a tabloid. Will everyone get it? Good, now you are off to a smart start. (More about crafting the perfect headline in Chapter 5.)

Your next task in appearing wise and knowledgeable is to keep things organized and moving. While preparing for your presentation, keep shuffling your modules until you feel the ideas clicking into place and connecting seamlessly. Use simple easy-to-track transitions. For example, if you are going to tell your audience three things, let everyone know you are going to tell them three things and then point to each item as it comes along in the speech: "first of all," "second," "lastly." If you are going to tell a story, alert them with, "Let me tell you a story." This kind of pointing will help listeners stay focused, or call them back from la-la land if they've drifted.

Finally, use your summary module to retell your audience what you've already told them and your call to action module to tell them what they are supposed to do with the information. If they leave your talk with a sense of forward motion and purpose, they feel smart. And here is the most beautiful part: When your listeners feel smart, they think you are smart. You can bask in the reflected glow of their high self-appraisal.

## The Fifth Grade Level

As I began writing this book, a new game show called *Are You Smarter than a 5th Grader?* debuted on TV, it recently was made into a board game. On the show, adults are asked questions about topics covered in grade school. If the adult is having difficulty answering the question, the adult can call on a fifth grader for help a maximum of three times.

The show helped me reinforce something I'd been telling my clients for years. Whenever they asked, "What level should I gear my message toward?" I'd tell them fifth grade. This is not to say you should dumb down your message. Fifth graders, as this TV show proved, are smarter than many of us think. But it is to say that you should:

- Keep your message simple and straightforward.
- Avoid obscure references.
- Never use an overly fancy, fussy word when a plain one will do.

Another thing fifth graders seem to be innately good at (I say innately because I don't think they actually offer a class in this in grade school) is detecting content that is full of bull. If you want to be thought of as sharp, be a matador—kill the bull.

*Details, Details: Believability Begins with Proof*

Next, let's look at the fear of not being believable. If you are afraid that you lack credibility, you simply need to become more credible. You should also consider that if this is your primary concern then probably the first person you need to convince is yourself.

The solution? Tackle your proofs module the way you prove your points with facts, stories, or analogies. First, look at your fact proofs. Are you really offering hard facts or mere generalizations? Are you being abstract or concrete? People may be skeptical if you say you are about to catch your competition unaware. So ask yourself, what is it you know? They *will* believe you if you know that your competitor's version of your new product has been on the drawing board for 2 years and is still 18 months from release. People may be dubious if you say you have an awesome advertising campaign. They will be convinced if you tell them the new slogan and reveal the ad placement schedule. Details, details, details are what add up to credibility.

Now look at your analogy and anecdote proofs. They are just the ticket for making abstract ideas more concrete. Be like those teachers who helped you to learn otherwise remote lessons—the law of gravity, algebraic equations, civil rights—by applying them to real-life experiences.

Bolstering your facts, anecdotes, and analogies will help you feel more credible and thus convey believability. What you believe inside radiates outside. Once you are sure you believe yourself, check your context module. You'll want it to offer a brief but sensible rationale for why you are a go-to source in your particular topic.

## To Build Credibility, End the Hyperbole

Exaggeration is the sworn enemy of credibility. If you have a little problem, classify it as such and not as the end of the world. Conversely, if you have a little piece of a solution to a big problem, don't oversell it.

A case in point: Recently, oil giant BP launched an experimental gas station called Helios House in Los Angeles. This filling station has eco-friendly architecture and features that help educate the public on environmental issues. The company's talking points included the signpost module "a little better" (BP even used that phrase on a billboard). In not claiming too much, the company avoided baiting critics who would have pounced on loftier assertions.

### Flexibility Builds Likeability

Many people also fear speaking because, deep down, they fear that they won't be liked. Many factors go into likeability, and we'll return to this subject in Chapter 6, which specifically addresses matters of speaking style. But the truth is no speaker can convey warmth, genuineness, and responsiveness if he is essentially operating on autopilot, reading a script word for word without eye contact.

Being totally wed to an immoveable, nonmalleable script will damage your likeability because inflexibility will reflect itself in your personal bearing. It will cause your body movements to be rigid (or nonexistent) and your words to sound forced and affected. Your tone will be flat and your eyes will be glued to your text (or perhaps to some distant point on the horizon). You will, quite simply, look like somebody that is too wrapped up in the perfection of his text to relate to and resonate with the audience.

When you have a flexible text—the kind that modules enable—you look looser and seem more approachable.

### Drawing a Blank

Now we come to the final fear—that a worst-case scenario will occur and you will be struck dumb. While I can't guarantee you that gnarly problems won't arise (who am I to argue with Murphy's Law?), I can promise you that preparation using the modular method will ensure that you are never speechless.

Let's look at a few situations that might potentially cause you to draw a blank:

1. **Time theft:** You are scheduled to speak at the big company meeting and the guy in front of you runs over. You are up

next and are told that you now have only 15 minutes instead of the 30 minutes you had planned so carefully.

What do you do? Most people would go into the express lane and speed read. Doing so would only ensure that all your hard work would go down the tube. After all, when you race down the proverbial speedway, you are more likely to stumble and swerve out of control—all of the things you fear most.

In order to combat time theft you should instead change the way you prepare. Most people time their presentation from beginning to end. The modular method allows you to time in parts. That makes it easier to edit at the last minute, to keep the meat and eliminate the trimmings. In doing so, be sure to keep your headline and conclusion; but consider abbreviating your context module and using only one or two message points—each with only one fact, one analogy, or one anecdote. Eliminate any blocks of information your rambling colleague has already covered. People will appreciate your brevity—especially in contrast to the previous speaker's long-windedness—and your audience will appreciate you all the more if you avoid redundancies.

2. **Line theft:** Speaking of redundancies, does this sound familiar? You are speaking on a panel or as part of a team. No matter how you've attempted to find out what the person before you is going to say, he says exactly what you were going to say.

That leaves you in the position of mumbling multiple iterations of "as Joan just said . . ." or "I agree with Bob." With modules at the ready, no one can steal your thunder and dilute your message. You will always have backups and alternatives. You can make a similar point, but with a different story, a new metric, a fresh perspective.

3. **Last-minute focus change:** Imagine you are about to deliver a presentation on your company's new customer service policy. The policy has to do with allowing for a longer window during which consumers can return the company's products and also offers free shipping for returns. You planned a talk that focuses equally on process adherence, status, and the competitive landscape.

Your general outline looks something like this:

| Opening (headline and context) | Message Point #1 Process Adherence | Message Point #2 Status | Message Point #3 Competitive Landscape | Conclusion (Summary and Call to Action) |
|---|---|---|---|---|
| | Facts (2 slides) | Facts (3 slides) | Facts (2 slides) | |
| | Anecdote (1 slide) | Analogy (2 slides) | Anecdote (3 slides) | |
| 3 minutes | 5 minutes | 5 minutes | 5 minutes | 2 minutes |

But just before the meeting, your CEO tells you that he is not interested in the details of process adherence—only status and competitive landscape. Since you used the modular method to prepare your speech, all you need to do is delete the unwanted data. If you choose, you can use the extra time to beef up your remaining modules. So, your final outline might look something like this:

| Opening (Headline and Context) | Message Point #1 Process Adherence | Message Point #2 Status | Message Point #3 Competitive Landscape | Conclusion (Summary and Call to Action) |
|---|---|---|---|---|
| | | Facts (3 slides) | Facts (5 slides) | |
| | | Analogy (4 slides) | Anecdote (3 slides) | |
| 4 minutes | | 7 minutes | 7 minutes | 2 minutes |

With moveable modules you can adjust your presentation to match the immediate needs of the audience and the situation.

## Fear of Fear Itself

If apprehension about speaking has long been a habit of yours, one other element that contributes to it is your fear of the fear. If someone even hints at the possibility that you might have to give a talk, you feel physically, mentally, and emotionally stressed.

Develop a strong presentation.

Write it down.

Practice.

Remember:

- When you did well.
- They are looking for information not a performance.

Start slow and simple.

Breathe deeply in through your nose. Hold. Breathe out slowly through your mouth.

Find the friendly faces.

**Figure 3.1   Fear Busters**

If this happens to you, I suggest that you fight that fear with some fear busters (see Figure 3.1).

Below are a few specific things I suggest you do right away to combat your fear.

### Remember Good History, Not Bad

Quite possibly, the prospect of speaking starts you down the road to remembering times you felt foolish in front of an audience, whether that was last week or as long ago as childhood. For me, it was that time when I was in a grade-school play. While reciting my lines, suddenly the elastic in my costume pants came loose and the pants fell in white puddles at my feet. (Talk about being caught with your pants down!) I couldn't understand why I was getting big laughs at such a somber moment. Obviously, I survived this trauma, but it took me a while to learn not to dwell on it. Now I take—and pass along—the sage advice offered by my son Matt's baseball coach. This former pro ball player suggested that Matt picture everything about his last win in order to win again.

In other words, when you are faced with speaking in public, think about a time you felt good about speaking in front of an audience. This can be any situation in which you felt comfortable and believed you were being effective, whether it was when you gave a toast at a family wedding, delivered a convincing argument to colleagues at work, or voiced a concern at a parent-teacher conference. Picture a win so that you can triumph once again.

### Write It Down

Another way to get rid of the fear of presenting information during a business meeting is to stop worrying about how you will deliver, and get busy writing the presentation. As soon as you catch yourself in apprehension mode, use that excessive jolt of energy to start scribbling. Instead of worrying about how you will be perceived or what could go wrong, begin jotting down your modules and filing them away.

Writing things down is just plain good preventative medicine for stage fright. Even if you know what you want to say to a particular crowd and you have a slide set that will prompt you for the bulk of the presentation, have a written text for that first all-important minute. Highlight or underline the important lines. You will feel calmer just knowing you can default to the words in case you suddenly become stricken with fear. Writing what you want to say helps your thoughts gel and you will remember better.

Winston Churchill—one of history's great orators (most of the time)—illustrated the importance of writing things down. He once got up to address Parliament, tired and stressed, and he went blank. Apparently he couldn't remember what he wanted to say on the important issue he was scheduled to address, so after a minute of looking confused and embarrassed he went back to his seat. His enemies reportedly made much fuss about his actions, but you only have to take his stage fright as a warning.

As news anchors, my colleagues and I were often required to ad lib, but no matter what our opening line was, it was always written down for us to read. Although for many years a television anchor begins the broadcast by saying, "Good evening everyone. In the news tonight . . ." that greeting has always been written out in the teleprompter for our reference.

Let your written modules serve as your calming touchstones. Nothing and no one can throw you off your game when you have anticipated all the moves.

## The Eighth Module

Okay, finally here it is: You probably can't dip into any book on speaking and presenting information without encountering a section on the importance of breathing. I thought of omitting it, since you have probably heard it before, but that really wouldn't be fair. It is so important that; it cannot be said enough.

In a way, breathing is the eighth module. It's an integral part of how we communicate. Even while trying to get out a torrent of words, we all have to breathe sometime. But if you are nervous, you are probably breathing out of the very top of your lungs. This is good enough to keep you alive (no small achievement in the grand scheme of things), but it is not enough to counteract fluttering pulses, sweaty brows, and racing thoughts. Deep breathing slows your heart rate, lowers blood pressure, and reduces adrenaline flow.

Before you begin speaking, try breathing through your nose, holding your breath for five seconds and breathing out through your mouth. If you lose your way while speaking, or even if you are in an emotional twist just contemplating speaking, repeat this breathing exercise. In the news business we learned to keep sentences short. This allows you to take breaths more often. There is nothing worse than trying to read long sentences and getting nervous because you know you sound breathless! In fact, why don't you try deep breathing a few times right now, before you turn the page? When you do turn it, you're going to learn a lot more about the nitty-gritty of delivering your news.

## Top Tips

1. Breathe deeply to start. Use shorter sentences to allow you to breathe more often throughout.
2. Write out your open and bring it with you as insurance against the jitters. Just don't plan on reading it!
3. Remind yourself that your audience is not there to judge performance; your listeners are just hoping to get news they can use and avoid boredom.

# PART

# II

# MESSAGE BOOT CAMP

# 4

# Audience

## THE "WHAT'S IN IT FOR ME?" PRINCIPLE

Every 16-year-old who has ever wanted to borrow the family car knows one thing for sure about making his pitch: You make it differently depending on which parent you are asking. With Mom, you share all the details, vow to call from each stop, and promise to wake her when you get home. Voilà, you get the Volvo. With Dad, your pitch is a bit different. You keep it short. You skip the details but promise to clear the driveway without even getting *close* to his beloved, fully restored, vintage Mustang convertible. You promise to make curfew and tiptoe in *without* waking him. Result, you get the keys—and maybe some money for gas.

As adults, we often fail to consider the different concerns and points of view of the people on the other end of our presentation or speech. Oftentimes, we don't take the time to find out what buttons need to be pushed in order to achieve the desired result. Because we fail to fine-tune our presentation to our audience, we ultimately fail to persuade the audience.

This chapter addresses the audience aspect—the who—of making professional presentations. Knowing your audience is the first thing I'll discuss in this section of the book because it is the first thing you need to address when planning a presentation. And that is true whether you will be addressing an audience of many or a key decision maker who is an audience of one.

Understanding and connecting with your audience is the key to getting what you want. Do you want the customer to buy what you are selling? Do you want your employees to perform better? Do you want the boss to green light your pet project? After you learn how to understand and connect with your audience, then—whether you are talking to a big group or a party of one—you must recognize that all audiences are not the same.

## Is Anyone Here but Me? Overlooking or Misunderstanding the Audience

Sadly, what we instinctively knew as a car-mooching high school kid—that we have to tailor what we say to the person hearing it in order to get our message across—appears to get lost in the shuffle by the time we enter the workforce. In the *Wall Street Journal Guide to the Top Business Schools 2006*, editor Ronald Alsop recounted an anecdote that illustrates this unfortunate truth.

The story involved Whirlpool Corporation, and cited Chris Aisenbrey, the appliance maker's director of global university relations. Aisenbrey explained that Whirlpool had grown so concerned about the lack of communication skills among business school graduates that it added a new assessment measure to its M.B.A. recruiting process; candidates were now asked to give 10-minute presentations of their resumes. Mr. Aisenbrey noted that while some candidates did a credible job, others did not consider what their potential employers needed to know. He said, "We see a lot of candidates who simply regurgitate their resume in chronological order. This is a simple case of candidates not understanding the audience and what message they want to send."

### Topping the List

Inferior communication skills topped a list of misgivings that recruiters voiced about M.B.A. students in the *Wall Street Journal*/Harris Interactive survey. The second complaint the recruiters registered was a lack of leadership skills. Not surprisingly, these top two grievances are related: Without exception, excellent leaders are excellent communicators. It's meaningless to have a vision unless that vision can be shared effectively.

Not understanding the audience . . . imagine that! Is it just because they're young and inexperienced? In part, many M.B.A. candidates are casualties of business school curricula that focus heavily on accounting, marketing, and strategy while giving scant attention to critical soft skills like communication. That said, a number of top business schools do stress communication skills—and *still* sometimes turn out graduates who don't appear to have learned the right lessons.

The truth is that novices and seasoned businesspeople alike often overlook the needs of the "other" in their communications for a multitude of reasons. When time pressures loom they tend to work backward and start pulling together *what* they'll say before thinking about *to whom* they'll say it. They ask only, "What slides do we have for this?" and "Can we get data to support that?" When they are "just too busy" they default to recycling: "Let's just pull that speech I gave to the Rotary Club last week . . . that'll be fine." Of course, it's *not* fine if the group you will address has other interests.

In addition, some speakers are simply too self-involved to think about the other guy. But if self-involvement is often the source of the problem, it can also—when flipped on its head—be the source of the solution. What speakers need to realize is that *everybody else is also self-involved*.

## WIIFM: What's In It for Me?

The International Listening Association (yes, there actually is such a thing) reminds us that most people will not really listen or pay attention to your point of view until they become convinced you have heard and appreciate their opinions. Another way of putting this is: If you want people to "get" you, they have to believe you have "gotten" them. They don't care how much you know until they know how much you care.

When people devote their time (no matter how briefly) and attention (even a sliver of it) to you, they feel entitled to get something back. This is not selfish per se; it is simply human nature. All relationships, social psychologists tell us, thrive or perish based on their ratio of benefits versus costs. We want to feel like we get at least as much as we give. The relationship between speaker and listener is like all relationships in this way. Listeners about to devote precious moments to listening want to know, "What's in it for me?" That's why any really good presentation begins with the presenter asking himself, "What's in it for my listener?"

### A Timeless Principle

When Aristotle said, "The fool persuades me with his reasons; the wise man persuades me with my own," he was, in his eloquent way, stating the WIIFM principle. If you want to persuade anyone to do anything, you must begin by knowing what motivates that person and what makes sense to them.

Let's get back, for a bit, to the task posed by Whirlpool recruiters. In asking job candidates to "tell us about yourself," what are they really asking? Unsuccessful candidates are, no doubt, the ones who take the task too literally. They try to cram as much self-referential material as possible into the allotted 10 minutes—the "more is more" approach: *I won the eighth grade spelling bee; I won the state high school swimming championship; My date and I were King and Queen of the prom.*

The successful job candidates, and prepared speakers, think about the assignment in a deeper way. Sure, recruiters for any organization want to know about applicants' backgrounds. But more specifically they want to know what special skills and knowledge the candidates bring to the table and why they are a good match for that particular industry and company. Moreover, they want some kind of assurance that job seekers are going to "bring it," that is, show up every day with enthusiasm and drive, and a hunger to learn all there is to know.

I recently coached a young man, Bobby, who was up for a job at the iconic music publication, *Rolling Stone*. It was his dream job. He came to me with the goal of connecting with his audience at the upcoming interview. In order to appeal to his audience of interviewers, who were, presumably, proud of their publication and interested in safeguarding its future, we focused his message around three key points.

1. Bobby referred to his lifelong love of the publication and backed it up with specific examples of memorable interviews and quotes ("the way the member of Cream dissed the drummer").
2. He cited articles he had written for his college paper that resonated with readers who also matched *Rolling Stone's* target demographic. In order to present this type of information, we conducted research that showed *Rolling Stone* did not want to be "your dad's music magazine."
3. He expressed his willingness to do anything—to work hard and bring his full focus to any and every assignment, no matter how small. I refer to this as a willingness to "work the street." In my NBC days I was unimpressed with interns who told me they wanted to be an anchor. I wanted to see someone who wanted to learn the ropes and actually cover the stories that they'd introduce as an anchor.

Job seekers often get hired when those who interview them believe they are not only qualified on paper but also genuinely interested in and committed to working hard in that particular field. Simply reciting one's credentials is just going through the motions.

Likewise, people get business when they can convince decision makers that their specific needs are understood and that these needs will not only be met but exceeded. To illustrate this point, I'll tell you about Lucy, who has owned a small executive search firm in San Francisco since the year 2000. Lucy had been doing very well, but came to me to help her do better, especially when pitching business to human resources executives. The meticulous, authoritative manner that made her a success in placing C-level executives didn't always sit well with folks who might feel they should be doing her job. Besides, some HR executives preferred relationships with big search firms that provided a bigger CYA (cover your, er, behind) factor than a boutique firm could. In other words, if a high-profile firm goofs up and gets you to hire a not-so-swift head of marketing—hey, you did *your* job. You worked with one of the biggest names in the business, and if they didn't get it right you're not to blame.

When Lucy ran through her standard pitch for me she started out by citing successful executives she had placed. Good. But then she did what so many people do wrong, that is, she launched, painstakingly, into her background. She talked about growing up in San Jose, and then went chronologically through her resume: advanced degrees in psychology and business, a big job at a bank, followed by a decade as a partner with one of the world's most prestigious search firms before launching her own firm. Not so good. Lucy's resume is impressive, and, if listeners connect the dots, suggests that her business and search experience, combined with a background in psychology, might give her deeper than usual insights into job candidates. But even so, her detailed resume doesn't belong at the beginning of her presentation.

Remember, HR executives want to know what is in it for them if they work with Lucy. They want to know what Lucy is doing now and why she does it better than others. I stopped Lucy from getting bogged down in her context module and moved a section where she differentiated her firm to the front of her presentation. For instance, she cited the fact that she conducts fresh research on every job candidate as opposed to larger firms that might use recycled bios in a data bank. Then, Lucy used selected facts from her resume (for example, her psychology background) as support for her firm's differentiators rather than as stand-alone accomplishments. Now her presentation was not so much about her as it was about meeting the needs of her audience.

## Audience *Always* Matters: Show Your Respect

Some executives fail to tune into their audience because they figure they don't need to persuade them. They are conducting a forced march. But this approach usually doesn't work. They will hear you but they may not follow. Furthermore, if you don't look for what really motivates the troops, your message won't be as strong, or have the impact you intended.

For example, I recently worked with Bill, the chief technology officer of a large company that includes many semiautonomous departments each with a technology team of its own to serve each department's unique needs. I was helping him prepare to talk to these tech teams to convince them that the business would be better if they pooled the teams into just one that would serve all the departments. For example, the technician who had been working solely in advertising might be assigned to a project with the financial services business one day and insurance the next. The big advantage for the company was that by pooling technicians into one big unit and dispatching them like SWAT teams to different departments, duplication of services would be avoided and this would save a lot of money.

In order to facilitate this organizational change, Bill had been doing the rounds internally at the executive level and with outside equity analysts who followed the company stock stressing the money savings message. But a savings message rarely, if ever, is a big motivator for employees. The change wasn't going to put any more money in *their* pockets.

When I asked Bill what employees thought of the initiative, he first indicated it didn't much matter because the decision had been made. *Fait accompli.* Okay, I said, but wouldn't it be helpful and wouldn't he be more successful if he could sweeten the idea for them. Yes! He thought about it and said the new system could make their current jobs more interesting. When I pushed further he added that the change would give technical team members a variety of experiences, help them become more savvy about the company, and develop more skills, something like cross training (like having basketball players box and swim in the off season). That potentially would give them more job security and job options outside the company. So, using the modular method, we tailored his presentation for tech employees:

- We kept Bill's headline: "The shared services initiative is the single biggest move the company has made in 20 years."
- But we revisited his three message points for executives and analysts: "Pooling our technology teams will save us money, improve customer service, and make us stronger competitors by improving innovation."
- We kept his message points about savings and progress, but moved them down in the presentation order. Instead, we led with the point: "This move means more job security for you, our employees."
- We added proofs (facts, analogies, and anecdotes) to support the job security subhead. For example, Bill did a day-in-life of a technician anecdote module and used personal quotes, where the technician described how much better her job was now. He also added a fact module about a business that had adopted the shared tech model and preserved everyone's job!

Bill's original call to action module for his tech staff had been: "We need your help to make this a success." We left it just as it was, because now it really made sense in terms of WIIFM. The staff knew exactly what was in it for them to get on board and bring enthusiasm to the new plan.

The speaker now did a much better job of connecting to his employee audience. In fact, the presentation's new points were so strong, he used them in presentations to audiences outside the company. After all if he had a strong pitch to employees, the business plan had a better chance of being successful.

## Do Your Due Diligence for WIIFM

Whether you are presenting in-house, out-of-house, to your staff, to your bosses, to your customers, to industry analysts, to recruiters, or to anyone at all, it is your job as a speaker to figure out who your audience is and what their interests are.

If you are a manager speaking at a plant far from the main office about a new initiative, you need to get on the phone ahead of time and find out what the local buzz is. Talk to supporters *and* critics. As a reporter, I learned that you need to ask more than you think you need to know because you never know when you'll get special insights that will give you an edge. If you are trying to persuade, sell, or impress—information is power.

If you are a CEO about to speak at a college or business school commencement, check out the school ahead of time. Find out what are the most popular classes and majors. Who are the favorite professors? What are the predominant political leanings? Are these the kind of grads who would want to work for you—and that you would want working for you?

If you are a salesperson making a pitch to a potential client, you need to research that client until you know virtually everything that can be known about him. An organization's web site is a good place to start researching, but it's not the be all and end all. Read press coverage, speak to people with firsthand knowledge, and go straight to the source whenever you can to discover how your clients see themselves.

Figure 4.1 offers a checklist of due diligence questions you should be addressing each time you prepare to give a talk.

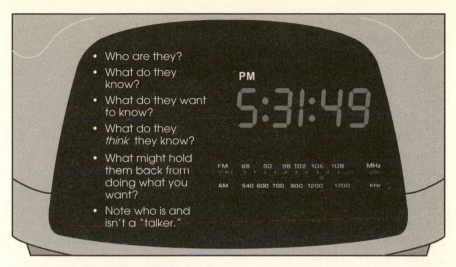

- Who are they?
- What do they know?
- What do they want to know?
- What do they *think* they know?
- What might hold them back from doing what you want?
- Note who is and isn't a "talker."

**Figure 4.1     Tune In to WIIFM**

I always try to practice what I preach. Before I begin coaching new clients, it's important to me that I understand how they rate themselves as speakers and what they want to work on. I send a questionnaire in advance, which in some ways is better than asking face-to-face questions because clients have more time to reflect on what their goals are rather than if I'd just asked at the start of a session.

## Asking the Right Questions

When I worked with top global corporate real estate salespeople, they shared the five essential questions to which they always found the answers before presenting to a potential buyer:

1. What does the buyer's balance sheet look like?
2. What is the buyer's business plan?
3. Who is the buyer's competition?
4. Where does the buyer have property?
5. Have we done deals with this buyer elsewhere and what was that experience like?

## An Audience of One: Matching Modules to Decision Styles

Finally, in discussing the importance of understanding and connecting to your audience, let's look at the dynamics of presenting to an audience of one when that one is the ultimate decision maker, such as a CEO.

In a two-year study of 1,600 executives across a variety of sectors, published in the *Harvard Business Review*, researchers found that managers too often use a one-size-fits-all approach in presentations. In addition, they found that half of all sales presentations are mismatched to the decision maker's style. They concluded that people can vastly improve their chances of having their proposals and pitches succeed by tailoring them to the decision makers' styles of thinking and behaving.

If everything depends on one person's decision-making style, you as presenter should try to ascertain what that is and then customize your approach. This is a critical part of WIIFM, because decision makers will not be able to hear what's in it for them unless you organize your presentation in a way that resonates with their preferences. As always, your message modules can help you tailor your pitch. For example:

> **Are you presenting to a magnetic leader with an inspiring vision?**
> Such people are often risk takers, although they also pride themselves on being responsible. They are easily intrigued by a good story but make their final decisions based on substance. They are interested in innovation, so a headline along those lines is often warranted, but be sure to follow up with business rationale in your subheads. Magnetic visionaries respond to simple, straightforward arguments, so don't load them down with data. Use your strongest metric to support each point, but list the bulk of your detailed data in a separate supplementary document. Since high-energy, magnetic types have relatively short attention spans, use visuals where you can. Be sure to sharpen and time your entire presentation, module by module. Now you can easily eliminate an anecdote or fact if the decision maker says, "Great, "I've got the idea and like it."

**Are you presenting to a risk-averse type who wants someone else to do the trail blazing?** For this type of leader, expand on your anecdote proofs, focusing on specifics about other respected organizations that have already done what you are suggesting. For factual support, call out examples of decisions this very leader has made in the past that would seem to support this suggested move.

**Are you presenting to a skeptical "show me" type who is suspicious of every data point?** Such people may take some risks, but they need to be thoroughly convinced. With them, your facts are critical, and your metrics need to be bolstered with support from credible experts and with case studies. Since this type tends to interrupt frequently, be extremely familiar with your modules and prepared to shuffle them on a dime. Be prepared to enlist ancillary support as well, for example by arranging for a call to a data source for verification.

**Are you presenting to a highly thoughtful, cerebral type?** Deep thinkers can go off on a tangent, so be prepared to expand on any of your modules as requested. Cerebral types are also natural synthesizers, so be well acquainted with how each of your supporting points relates to the others.

Whatever the decision maker's style, it's important not only that you understand it but also that you respect it—and that the decision maker senses your respect. Familiarize yourself with the decision maker's successes. Show enthusiasm. Don't waste your time wishing for a different kind of audience. Work with the audience you've got, and help them see what's in it for them.

---

**Top Tips**

1. Think like a reporter. Ask more than you think you need to know about your audience's attitudes and interests before presenting.
2. Connect to your audience as soon as possible.
3. When presenting to a key decision maker—an audience of one—take that individual's personal decision style into account.

# CHAPTER 5

# Substance

## WHAT'S YOUR HEADLINE?

Whether a train has derailed, the president shakes up his cabinet, or a new Hollywood celebrity baby arrives, every newscast starts off the same way: The anchorperson briefly greets viewers and then delivers the headlines, usually one-line summaries of three top stories. These headlines, or teasers, are offered right up front with good reason: They let people know what information, out of all possible stories, is considered to be the most important or interesting right now.

If the headline is delivered correctly—clearly, concisely, and colorfully, with a bit of a tantalizing hook—people will feel that the more detailed news ahead is worth the wait. They'll stick around, even if it means waiting out toothpaste commercials, weather updates, and traffic helicopter shots of jackknifed tractor-trailers.

When I work with clients who are getting ready to speak, I always ask the same first question: "What's your headline?" To this, many people reply, "Hmm, that's a good question."

Then it dawns on them: They don't know the answer.

They have no idea what they should tell their audience right up front—in the first 30 seconds when listeners are most alert and receptive. Going in, they don't know what they want to leave 'em with. As a result, they miss opportunities to make an impact.

You can avoid this problem by paying careful attention to this chapter. It will focus on one module only—the headline—because the headline is such a critical element of any presentation.

## Ignoring the Elephant: Three Reasons People Miss Their Headline

As astonishing as it might seem, even senior executives and experts, people who *expect* to be listened to and remembered, can be oblivious to what their headline is. It's as if there's an elephant sitting on the podium beside them and they've decided to talk about everything but the elephant—"Gosh this stage is sagging!" "Have you noticed all the hay?"—but not that preeminent pachyderm. If sophisticated pros can miss something so obvious, anyone can. So it's worth understanding just why it is that so many people—and maybe you—avoid doing something so essential.

1. **We're afraid of oversimplifying:** Sometimes we feel that our topic is too complex or too important to summarize briefly. We think that if we do so, we might not be perceived as particularly erudite. But remember: The most important, complex events in modern history have all been reported to the public by journalists who introduced the stories with headlines. There is nothing simplistic about crafting a headline that can be quickly and easily understood. In fact, many people consider this a kind of art form.

    I recently worked with a leading doctor in California who was preparing a speech for a lay group of patient advocates. He was about to deliver a convoluted, technical summary of a recent study. When I pushed him to create a headline that explained what the study showed in simple terms, as he'd explained it to his individual patients, he balked. He feared he would lack credibility.

    A similar episode occurred with a leading partner in a Wall Street firm who was in charge of opening an office in India. Because many firms were already there, he wanted to tell reporters that his firm's differentiator was "securitization." It turned out to mean something pretty straightforward: Securitization is a way that lenders can get their capital back quickly by selling debt to investors. Initially, he didn't want to say that. He thought he would seem less credible.

Both the doctor and the Wall Street partner were self-conscious about simplifying because, as they each admitted to me in the end, they were imagining the scornful reactions of their own professional peers. Never mind that their professional peers were not who they were speaking to! In both cases, simplicity was precisely what was called for, considering their audiences. Simplicity enhanced credibility and authority because it enhanced accessibility of the message. The last thing a group of patient advocates wants is to be bombarded with obtuse medical terminology. The last thing journalists want is to be deluged with insider terminology that will leave their readers or viewers scratching their heads. In the end, most audiences, even those composed of consummate fellow professionals, value a simple, straightforward lead-in. Think about it: Even the most esoteric professional journals introduce their articles with short, intriguing headlines.

2. **We just don't recognize what is most important or interesting:** Many of us plan to speak without having asked ourselves the all-important question: What's the most important message I want to get across? We have a lot of points and figure we'll just roll them all out (probably talking way too quickly in an attempt to get them all in). We'll just let the listeners decide what is most significant.

   I call this "the Greek diner approach." If your menu is loaded with not just moussaka, but also lasagna, chow mein, crepes, and cheeseburgers, your customers might pick a dish that isn't your chef's best. You want to be the bistro with a few select dishes, so your diners will have no choice but to select quality. *You* need to know what's most important. Tell your audience what they should focus on and what they should remember.

---

### It All Started When . . .

Many business speakers think they should begin every talk with the history of their company. Sometimes this is relevant and necessary, but usually more than a few remarks along these lines will bore everyone but the two or three people who started with "a little garage space

*(Continued)*

and a big dream" (and sometimes even them). Would a reporter announce a World Series victory by leading with how the winning team came together? In general, people care less about the past than the present, and only about the future as it relates to them.

I recently worked with the founder of one of the world's largest candle companies. His company had created custom candles under various store brand names but now wanted to market its own brand. He planned to present to a group of reporters from *W, Elle, Vogue,* and *HG,* by starting with how he'd grown up in India, moved to the United States to go to college, and started his company—literally—in his garage with a candle he made in a Campbell's soup can.

Instead we started him off with a strong statement, "You may not have heard of us, but you probably have our candles; every day, two hundred thousand of our candles are sold in Targets, Saks and Nordstroms across the United States."

3. **We don't want to get into trouble:** A former *Wall Street Journal* reporter and colleague once noted that nowadays, "Everyone wants to be quoted but no one wants to say anything." Sometimes the absence of a clear, enticing headline is due to a fear of vulnerability. Many speakers equate saying anything substantive with going out on a limb. From this precarious perch, we might be challenged, criticized, perhaps even sued.

I'm not going to dismiss such fears out of hand. Anyone who's been paying the remotest attention to the zeitgeist knows that we live in a hypersensitive culture where a bold, decisive remark might draw some flak. But the downside of delivering a vague message filled only with platitudes, diluted truths, or recycled facts far outweighs the risk of a bit of audacity or even controversy. The simple fact is that if you go out of your way not to say anything significant, your message will lack any kind of power or "stickiness."

I was working with the head of a financial firm's exchange traded funds (ETFs). ETFs are similar to mutual funds but growing fast in popularity because of certain advantages. After a lot of thought, my client said her headline would be, "ETFs can play a role in most people's portfolios." This modest statement seemed at odds with his enthusiasm. I asked

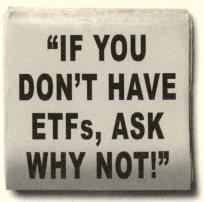

**Figure 5.1    Picture It In the Paper**

her to go out on a limb and just say what she really thought. We came up with, "All investors should be using ETFs. If not, they should be asking why not." (See Figure 5.1.)

Which headline would get you interested?

---

### I Don't Know What to Say . . . Yet

Sometimes we won't choose a decisive headline because we are not yet certain what it is we really want to say about a particular topic. If you happen to be the chairman of the Federal Reserve, you can make big news by saying, "I don't know yet about those interest rates." If you are *not* the Federal Reserve chairman, don't try anything like that.

If you really don't know what your headline is because you haven't made up your mind one way or the other, don't fudge it. Talk about something you *are* sure of.

---

## Writing Your Headline: Finding the "Aha"

Finding a headline is, as I've said, something of an art form. For anyone who's not used to formulating headlines, I can tell you from a reporter's perspective that the task is part cerebral and part gut instinct. You'll have to use your head and, to some extent, your intuition.

Sometimes big news is obvious, because it represents a breaking development: "CEO Dies of Apparent Heart Attack," or "Rookie Breaks Babe Ruth's Record." But lots of times the gold nugget requires some mining.

One thing that's fascinating about headlines is that in virtually every situation where professional reporters from various news outlets all attend the same speech, event, or courtroom trial they all emerge with the same basic headline. For example, consider two presidential press conferences with George W. Bush. In one, President Bush commented, almost as an aside in response to a question about immigration, that everyone in America should be required to learn English. *Aha!* In a second press conference, President Bush responded in the negative to a question about whether he would see Al Gore's film about global warming. *Aha!*

What did the reporters' instincts tell them about these two pieces of information? For one thing, they both concerned topics that were already on people's radar. Immigration is an issue that won't go away, and global warming—no pun intended—is hot. Both comments were also bound to incite a lot of emotion and pro and con discussion. Moreover, both had "legs," meaning that the stories would generate more buzz—and hence more stories—about possible forthcoming changes: Should English be declared our one official language? Should we abandon bilingual education? Are other Republicans planning on spurning the Gore film? Finally, both comments were significant because they were made in an almost offhand manner by the president. They were not necessarily what people were expecting to hear. They had an element of surprise.

When writing your headline or finding your own "aha!" statement, follow these three steps:

1. Make sure the topic excites you. If it doesn't excite you, it won't excite anyone else.
2. Ask yourself: Of all the facts or ideas that relate to my topic, which *one* surprises, amuses, reflects change, or represents actual news?
3. Ask yourself: What do I want to leave 'em with? Which idea or fact is most likely to instigate discussion and get, or keep a buzz going?

When you think you have a keeper, subject your headline to the "teaser test." Will it make your audience hungry for the meat on the bones that you will provide as you fill out your message? Headlines should "tell 'em what you're gonna tell 'em," but that's not all: They also have to give your listeners a reason to stay tuned.

### Tell Me More, Now!

A manager in charge of a sales incentive bonus program at a large multinational corporation was giving a presentation designed to promote cross selling. When a sales rep from one division met with a customer, that rep could receive a $1,000 bonus for providing a sales lead to a rep in another division if the information resulted in new business. It took about 10 minutes to do the necessary paperwork. The manager's perfect teaser headline: "Who here would like to make $100 a minute?"

By the way, did you note that this grabber was posed in question form? Play with your headline to see if asking it instead of telling it offers more of a hook.

## Think Like an Ad Writer

Once you've got your message ready for an outing, don't forget to dress it up. Why say, "We manufacture fantastic candles at a great price," when you can say, "No one can hold a candle to our candles"? To help dress your message, think like an advertising copywriter. Advertisers are great with headlines because they have to tell entire stories in the time it takes to flip a magazine page or drive by a billboard at 55 miles per hour.

I have a lot of friends in advertising, and I asked some of them how they get to the point so efficiently. Dennis Berger, former vice chairman and creative director of BBDO (Batten, Barton, Durstine & Osborn) created General Electric's "GE brings good things to light," wrote the Burger King jingle, and came up with Delta's "We love to fly and it shows." He says he always starts by asking the client how they think people see their brand and how they want them to see it. He also says it's important to stay honest and focus on what you're doing, not what you're going to do.

Janet Lyons, also a BBDO top creative executive working on the Pizza Hut, Federal Express, and Oral B campaigns, says her best ideas come from talking to employees about their jobs—in other words by going straight to the source. For example, when Janet worked with FedEx she talked to a middle manager about training employees. The manager said, "Sometimes I tell the people who work for me that there could be gold in any one of those packages." Janet used this as the foundation of "the golden package" campaign. It was a vivid image that elicited emotion by emphasizing the care FedEx employees take.

## What to Avoid in a Headline

Now you know what goes into a headline. But it's also important to know what to leave out. Remember, people's brains are overcrowded. In order for them to pass along a headline, that headline has to be free of language that weighs it down. So, avoid at all costs:

- **Overly complex words:** Are you about to "operationalize a paradigm shift by rolling out a solution to capture mindshare going forward?" Well, good luck with that. But you'll probably do better to craft your headline in plain English: "Our new product will change the way people think about X." (X being anything from golf balls to laser surgery to retirement planning—just be sure you say it so that people can understand it.)

### Say What?

I'll never forget an episode that took place when I worked at CNBC. A leading financial services firm put out a press release—positive news about its strong performance. The release was read aloud on CNBC and the first question the reporter asked the chief financial officer was, "What the heck does this mean?" With that, the value of all the company's good news diminished.

A Home Depot executive was on T.V. talking about the reasons his company had increased revenues, and he repeatedly attributed the increase to store "resets." When asked what reset meant he hemmed and hawed. He failed to simply explain that they'd rearranged their stores making things easier to find and reach.

- **Insider terms:** If you've been in an industry for a long time, you've doubtless gotten used to many of its shorthand terms and acronyms. Don't ever get so used to them that you don't notice when you're using them with people who do not understand. Your audience will be left in the dark and, worse, *you'll* be the one who appears out of touch with people you are trying to reach!
- **Hyperbole:** Headlines need to stand on their own as statements of fact. Puffing them up with exaggeration detracts from credibility. If you can't follow through with what you say in your headline, your message will register as a bait-and-switch routine. Question seriously any adjective you are tempted to place in your headline. Often they are unnecessary. (Mark Twain was not far wrong when he advised, "If you catch an adjective, kill it.") Steer especially clear of hyperbole like "premier," "world class," and "powerhouse." These words are not just exaggerations, they're clichés. And unless you're Paul Revere, think carefully before you announce anything "revolutionary."
- **Old or ho-hum news:** Do most people already know the news in your headline? Then find another headline, or put a new twist on the one you have.
  Everyone knows that the bull market in real estate is over, but do they know which areas still have rising prices?
  Everyone knows that it's hard to get into a selective college, but do they know that many of today's top CEOs did not attend Ivy League schools?
  If you don't have anything new to report, put a new spin on the news that's out there. Think about something you just read. Think about someone you just talked to. Then make a contemporary connection.

- **Big numbers for their own sake:** Finally, don't pad your headlines with big numbers for their own sake. Big numbers are not necessarily the most significant numbers. It is often the smaller metrics that suggest the biggest change, and hence the biggest news.

### Small But Significant

I recently worked with a speaker from a financial services firm who was preparing a presentation using data drawn from a poll of affluent investors. In talking about the increasing interest in emerging markets, he planned to highlight the fact that wealthy investors were most interested in China and India. This, however, was news to no one. A much smaller but significant number of those investors expressed interest in Malaysia. Now he had his surprising headline, one that would keep people listening and send the message that his firm had insights that we wouldn't necessarily find in the local newspaper's business section.

## Linking Your Headline to Other Modules

Your headline is the first message module you should develop. Everything else flows from it. Once you have your headline, you can use it to structure the remainder of your message modules.

The first thing you'll want to do is reinforce your headline with three message points that prove or support your main message. The three points have to be repeated. That doesn't mean repeating them verbatim like a broken record or a scratched CD. Repetition is achieved by expressing those three points in three different ways. For each point you look for a metric or a quote from an outside party (your fact module), a colorful comparison (your analogy module), and an engaging story or specific, granular example (your anecdote module).

The variety with which you express your points better ensures, your ideas will resonate with different types of people.

This 3 × 3 formula is of utmost use in getting people to remember what you say. Think of it as:

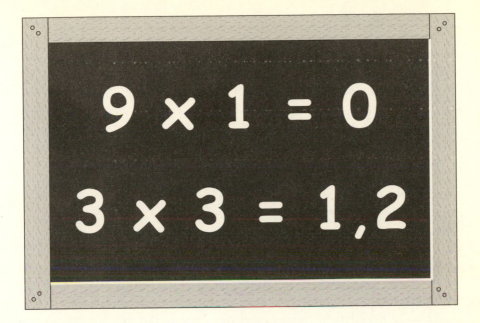

$$9 \times 1 = 0$$

$$3 \times 3 = 1{,}2$$

Translation: If you make nine points and deliver them only once, people will remember *not one thing* you've said by the end of the week. Make three points three ways, however, and they will remember at least one or two, and you come out ahead.

### What's My Story?

What people tend to remember best are well told stories from presentations. For this reason, anecdotes are the most important proof point. Yet they are the modules which give people the most trouble. Some can't think of a specific example, others aren't sure they can share it, and still others aren't sure how to make it interesting. In the upper echelons of the business world, these difficulties often stem from the fact that the people doing the public speaking may not be involved with customers at very basic levels.

When clients have trouble coming up with examples, I ask them to pretend they are directing their advertising team, telling *them* where to go to capture a picture of what they want to promote. I ask, "Where would you send the video crew, what would they see, and how does it represent a change or improvement over the way things used to be done?" Asking yourself to think this way can help you come up with a salient, memorable anecdote.

For example, I was working with a San Jose hotel owner who wanted to build business by promoting how they had added access to affordable golf. That was great, but he needed to paint a picture. He offered an anecdote: "A guest arrived a day before a big meeting. She'd planned to just wander around town alone. Instead we helped her squeeze in some great golf. We shuttled her to a top club for nine holes at a bargain price." You *pictured* this bored business woman who found a fabulous afternoon of golf, so you are more likely to *remember* why you should book that hotel next trip.

In addition to working with your $3 \times 3$ formula, you'll need to embellish your primary headline with a bit of *context*. This might involve what's happened already, that is, historical context. It might refer to what others are doing, or why you made the move you made.

Next, you'll need to work on your *signpost*—a brief refrain meant to resonate in listeners' minds. Your signpost might well turn out be a portion of the headline, or slightly different words that echo its essence.

Lastly, you'll want a *call to action*. Now that you've delivered your news, what is it you want your listeners to *do*? Don't shortchange yourself here. This is your payoff—the return you will get on your investment of the time and energy to think your presentation through, from the headline forward.

## Headline Study: A Public Relations Director

To give you a sense of how I worked with a client to generate a headline and connect other modules to it, I'll share this example:

Cynthia was a newly appointed public relations director at a New York-based magazine geared toward affluent males. She had two days to pull together a presentation for the entire ad sales team. A lot was riding on her success.

Like many new hires, Cynthia's inclination was to immediately fire up a PowerPoint with her biographical data. Instead, I suggested she think about the audience and what they wanted.

"They want to sell more ads," Cynthia said, without hesitation. So her headline became:

Good PR Results in News You Can Use to Win New Clients

We knew that would get the attention of her listeners because there was something in it for them.

After her headline, Cynthia continued, "Over the next twenty minutes I'm going to show you how our PR department, which has doubled the media mentions of our magazine, intends to keep our momentum going." Here came her three message points: "We have a new strategy that promotes our brand in everything from iPods to blogs, gets more ROI on 'cover boys,' and generates more buzz from news events."

Because Cynthia was new, she needed to briefly establish her credibility. So she quickly gave a bit of biographical context by describing her relevant experience. Then she quoted the publisher's goal for the magazine to "reach the elusive affluent male." She parenthetically pointed out how that goal happened to align with her own personal goal. This won hearty laughs from this young, hip audience (up went her likeability).

After her quip, Cynthia worked in a signpost by saying, "Seriously, good PR is news you can use." (Note how this signpost appropriated part of her headline.)

Now, Cynthia was ready to put some meat on her opening headline and embellish her three key supporting points.

1. **She planned to promote the brand using everything from iPods to blogs.** Here she offered *facts* about the increased number of media outlets, from podcasts to blogs to T.V. channels. She relayed an *anecdote* about a network T.V. segment done by one of the magazine writers and how an ad sales rep used that spot to win over a client who'd been ready to drop its business. She also used an analogy, saying this writer's appearance put "fuel in the sales rep's tank."

2. **She planned to improve the return on investment the magazine spent on celebrity "cover boys."** Here, Cynthia gave a metric (*fact*) about magazine sales in relation to the popularity of its cover models, told a story (*anecdote*) about wooing one well-known celebrity to be featured on the cover, and described the cluster of agents trying to get their clients on the cover by comparing the agents' excitement to that of kittens chasing a laser pointer (*analogy*).

3. **Public relations would work with marketing to coordinate buzz around events.** Here Cynthia used *fact*, *analogy*, and *anecdote* to describe how PR and sales would work hand in glove with regard to parties, press conferences, contests, and the like. She also managed to work her signpost in again.

Cynthia concluded with a summary and then a *call to action,* by motivating ad sales reps to communicate with her. She told her audience, "Public relations needs your support so we can support you better. We'll be calling you every couple of months to find out how you've used the news that PR has generated. We also hope you'll let us know where else we can help you. We can and will find that elusive, affluent male—together."

## Freshening Your Headline

Once you have your headline integrated with basic modules, you are good to go. What's more, you already have a jumpstart if you are asked to present your basic talk in a wide variety of situations. For example, Cynthia could have easily modified her talk for her publishing company's executives or for magazine distributors by shuffling her modules around and slotting in a few new facts, anecdotes, or analogies. But the first thing she would have to do when gearing up for a new audience would be to freshen up her headline. If she wanted to update an advertiser, her headline might be, "Our successful P.R. campaigns have helped put our magazine and your ads in the hands of more of the people you want to reach."

In fact, any speaker can easily tailor his headline to new audiences and new occasions by using a T.V. reporter's trick known as "freshening it for the 11." The phrase refers to putting a new spin on a story for the 11 P.M. broadcast.

Our viewers who tuned in for late-night news didn't want leftovers, even if the facts of our lead stories hadn't changed all day—and they often hadn't. The mayor's press conference had been held at noon and he wasn't coming out with any new information. The train wreck had occurred just after dawn and there wouldn't be a reenactment. The parade was over, St. Paddy revelers had gone home, and all that was left were party hats on the curb. Yet the producer needed the viewers to feel as though they were getting more than a rerun.

## The Solutions

"Tonight the president of the City Council said the Council would back the mayor's proposal announced this morning . . ."

"The Number 6 express train line remains closed tonight while investigators scour the tracks . . ."

"All that remains on Fifth Avenue tonight are faint traces, but people are still talking about one of the grandest parades . . ."

Getting "used news" feels like getting a fruitcake that's obviously been re-gifted. But by simply tweaking the headline you can get your audience to sense they are not getting a retread. They're getting something new, fresh, and customized.

You can freshen up your headline with material from any up-to-date source: today's newspaper, a story you heard from someone at breakfast, a reaction you got from an employee the last time you spoke. The point is to let the audience know that your message is relevant to what's happening now and what they care about at this moment.

Once your headline is freshened, it's time to look at your other modules and see if they could also use tweaking to support your up-to-the-minute message. But in some instances you might just find that simply changing your headline will be enough to do the trick. That's how powerful the right headline can be.

Whatever your news, whatever your message, focusing on your headline is, without a doubt, the most effective way to shape it. Whatever the occasion, your headline module will be indispensable. Procrastinators, please note: Asking, "What's my headline?" isn't something you can put off until tomorrow. It's something you must do *now*.

---

### Top Tips

1. Before every presentation ask, "What's my headline?"
2. Can you picture your headline in the paper?
3. Make sure *you* are interested in your headline topic; if you're not, no one else will be.

# CHAPTER 6

# Style

## "V" IS FOR . . . VISUAL, VOCAL, AND VERBAL

In this chapter I'll discuss what habits of style you should be cultivating as a speaker and which ones you should avoid. These three Vs really can mean the difference between indifference and victory in your communication. But before, we get into them, let me start by telling you a story.

My client Jim, a partner in a big accounting firm, had a mission in his speaking engagements. He wanted to talk about how accountants work honestly and responsibly, and really earn their money. He was trying to improve the image of a profession badly battered by scandals about improprieties over the past few years. Unfortunately, Jim had a habit of jangling his big, solid gold diamond-studded Rolex watch as he spoke. He didn't realize it, and didn't realize how damaging it was to his message, until I videotaped him. Then he immediately understood something was wrong.

Why didn't someone tell Jim that his physical appearance and body language were causing people to doubt the sincerity or validity of the information he conveyed during his presentation? Perhaps everyone was being polite. Perhaps it seemed nitpicky. Perhaps people couldn't pinpoint exactly *why* they didn't believe him—they just knew they didn't.

The problem was that Jim's style clashed with the substance of his speech. When that happens the audience believes what they see more than what they hear.

How do we know this? A famous series of studies by UCLA psychology professor Albert Mehrabian showed that face-to-face communication—especially the kind that involves communicating about emotions or attitudes—relies on three elements: words, tone of voice, and body language.

Specifically, Professor Mehrabian's study found that when it comes to communications about attitudes or emotions, listeners unconsciously weigh factors differently in determining a speaker's believability. The cues they rely on are listed in Figure 6.1.

Now here's the really important part: When emotions or attitudes are being communicated by a speaker whose words are in conflict with nonverbal cues, listeners are more apt to give the latter much more weight. In other words, my client Jim could opine all he wanted about the upstanding nature of his profession; his big, swinging Rolex caused people to doubt his sincerity.

### Let's Go to the Videotape

Most of my clients discover disturbing quirks of style only after viewing a videotape of themselves—on the other hand, videotape can be a confidence builder. Bottom line, I highly recommend this practice, along with that of rehearsing in front of someone who will give you honest feedback about your strengths and your challenges.

Don't let what happened to Jim happen to you. Take style seriously! Based on Professor Mehrabian's seminal study, I've divided my style advice into three main areas: visual, vocal, and verbal. Each element is vitally important. Now, let's get to the three Vs.

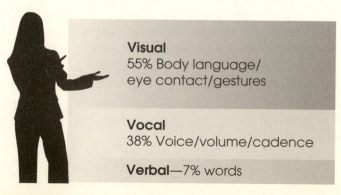

**Visual**
55% Body language/
eye contact/gestures

**Vocal**
38% Voice/volume/cadence

**Verbal**—7% words

**Figure 6.1   Style Sells**

## "V" #1: Visual Elements

In this section we'll look at a number of things that contribute to our visual style, including gestures, smiles, and eye contact. We'll look at the importance of how you enter a room and of how you move within that room. In short, we'll see how what you do with your body affects how people hear what comes out of your mouth.

Body language provides the audience clues to the meaning and intent of what you are saying. It is a source of communication that is often more reliable in telling us what is really going on than the words themselves. Although studies verify this, the truth is all of us know it instinctively. We don't need a Ph.D. in the social sciences to realize that when someone says, "I'll call you," while looking away, frowning and shrugging their shoulders, our phone is not going to ring. Or, when your family says, "Yes, Mom this is just delicious," as they scoot the food around the plate or feed it to the dog under the table, they really hope you lose that recipe. In many cases, actions speak louder than words.

As I was trying to get to the top of the heap as a reporter, I spent a lot of time putting together audition tapes of my best stories and newscasts that put my skills on display. Once I finally reached New York City, a seasoned news director told me that he screens such tapes on mute, looking for the people who would make him *want* to listen. Talk about the power of the visual.

### Making Your Entrance

Let's start with first things first. Before you speak, you've got to get to the place, seat, or podium where you'll be speaking, so you might as well make the right entrance. After all, the easiest way to gain instant credibility is to take advantage of your all-important first few minutes in front of your audience.

Straighten up and stride confidently to the front of the room. Say hello and . . . pause. Look down briefly to organize your materials. When you look up, smile (glancing down always gives you a chance to "change moods" without being jarring—and you can do this throughout your presentation).

Now here's a trick that a teacher friend of mine taught me: If a couple of people continue chattering, simply look at them and pause. This will usually get them to settle down. It might take a few seconds for them to realize they're on your radar screen, but once they realize you are signaling your intent to start your presentation, they will pay attention.

### Smile . . . at Least for a While

Smiling is one of the most powerful communication tools that we can use. An innate response, smiling begins in early infancy and is a critical factor in helping parents bond with a baby. For the rest of our lives, smiling factors into social bonding and enhances our likeability.

Smiling can help you influence people even when it appears the odds are stacked against you. For example, studies indicate that a nice smile is one of our main criteria for electing U.S. presidents. And according to Daniel McNeill, author of *The Face: A Natural History*, although courtroom judges are likely to find smilers and nonsmilers guilty in equal numbers, they give smilers lighter penalties: a phenomenon known as the "smile leniency effect."

Yet, oftentimes speakers fail to use the best arrow in their quiver. In some cases, they just don't know how important smiling is or they simply don't realize they're not smiling. But in many cases, they believe there is nothing to smile about. I say, that is almost never the case.

I do a lot of work in the financial industry, where you might think that hard metrics would matter most when it comes to feeling positive about a presenter. But I once did a survey of stock analysts to find out what mattered most to them when it came to presentation style. Based on the survey results, I concluded that "likeability" ranked high on the list; and what better tool to use to increase one's likeability than a simple smile. That piece of information came in handy when I worked with Greg, the head of private equity at a big bank.

Although I've now worked with Greg many times over the years, I remember the first time best because I thought I'd blown the relationship before it began. Every year Greg had to deliver a presentation to one of the toughest audiences—his big institutional investor clients (guys who, if they aren't happy, will put their zillions of dollars somewhere else). He did a dress rehearsal for me of the presentation where he had to spell out his wins and losses. Greg did a good job of presenting his platform, but he didn't come across as likeable. The fact is, Greg isn't a warm and fuzzy kind of guy.

He seems like he came out of central casting to promote Gordon Gecko's "greed is good" ethic.

Greg needed everything he could muster to assure his audience that he was not slick but sincere. He needed to convince them he'd continue to give it his all and that he was the best they'd find anywhere.

I told my new client, "Greg you don't come across as very likeable." He quickly responded, "Oh, I know. I just don't know what to do." When I suggested that he simply smile, Greg said there was nothing to smile about. He certainly didn't want to smile at inappropriate times, which is perfectly understandable. As a result, we had to work in some content that was smile-worthy. We added a colorful story about a real character who finally decided to sell the family business to the firm over a gaggle of other suitors. We also added a story about Greg's son's struggles as a catcher (most of his listeners had kids and we knew they could relate).

Finding a place to smile during a business presentation also worked for one of my British CEO clients. I mention his nationality because we Americans seem to have many preconceptions about the British. For some reason, we think they are smarter than we are, but we also think many of them are stiffer and possibly somewhat less likeable. Tony Blair had Americans bowled over in part because he came across as intelligent *and* humorous. He had a ready smile. And so, as it happened, did my client. But when I asked him why he didn't use the radiant smile he'd used to help him get to the top, he said his presentations rarely gave him the opportunity. Recently named the top executive, he was having to make a lot of unpopular moves to restore his company's profitability.

As usual I could relate to his conundrum. When I first started out as a newscaster the most irritating feedback I would get from friends and complete strangers was, "Why don't you smile more?" I would remind them that most of the time, the stories I was reading were not pleasant, let alone amusing. (The only reason to smile while reading about a big fire is if you refer to a firefighter as a "firefarter" as I mistakenly did one time on-air and no one has let me forget!) But as I came to understand, there are places in the newscast to smile, to laugh, and show your humanity. A good producer makes sure those opportunities to smile come periodically in a 20-minute news broadcast—and so should you in your presentations.

As for the British CEO, he created one or two lighter moments in his speech. Then I told him to be sure to glance down and glance up again when shifting moods and modes. As I do with many of my clients, I took a copy of his speech and literally wrote "SMILE" on it at the appropriate moments so he would not forget.

---

### Mood Altering

In the typical newscast, even if most of the news is grim, newscasters tend to smile at the open, at the commercial breaks that come roughly 7 and 14 minutes into a 30-minute newscast and when they sign off. The trick is to glance down and use a few choice words to help change moods. Be sensitive. One of the worst things a producer can do is read a story about a tragic death and then tease the dog show that's in town. You know that has happened when you hear the anchor say, "On a much lighter note . . ."

---

### Look Them in the Eye

Eyes are often called "windows of the soul," yet too many speakers keep the curtains closed when they get up in front of an audience. If you stare at your slides or your text you may not miss a word but your audience will miss the message. Making eye contact with your listeners is important. It says you are confident. It says you care about everyone in the audience.

When speaking to a small group, look briefly from one person to another. For a larger audience, mentally divide the room into three parts. During various parts of your talk, find what seems to you to be a friendly face in each group and make eye contact with that person. Don't allow your eyes to dart around, and don't neglect the far sides of the room.

When you have text or slides to read, look for and mark parts where you can most easily establish eye contact without losing your train of thought. As a reporter who had to do live shots, with little preparation and lots of specific information to relate, I learned that eye contact was easiest to make on the first and last lines of each paragraph. It also has the effect of making the audience feel as though you have memorized more than you have. The lines on which you make contact needn't be long lines, but the words do need to be simple and easy to say.

In Figure 6.2, I have included extract from the commencement address that Steve Jobs gave to the graduating class of Stanford University in 2005. As discussed in Chapter 2, Jobs' speech was praised by people throughout cyberspace because it provided graduates with inspirational and meaningful advice. I have marked up this text in the way I would for a client who was preparing to make a speech. The text that is written in bold, the words that I underlined, and the notes written in parentheses are directive comments that would let the speaker know when to make eye contact with the audience, to emphasize a word, or to walk away from the podium in order to engage the audience.

**(SMILE–Divide eye contact between 3 points below)**

I am honored to be with you today ...

at your commencement ...

from one of the finest universities in the world.

**(GLANCE DOWN THEN UP)**

I never graduated from college. Truth be told, this is the closest I've ever gotten to a college graduation. Today I want to tell you three stories from my life. That's it. No big deal. Just three stories. **(Gesture 3 then 1)**

The first story is about connecting the dots.

**(Walk 3 steps to side of podium)**

I dropped out of Reed College after the first 6 months, but then stayed around as a drop-in for another 18 months or so before I really quit. So why did I drop out?

**(Note: I underline words to stress and italicize words on which to change tone)**

This approach has never let me down, and it has made *all the difference* in my life...

**Figure 6.2    Mark Your Moves**

Next time you prepare to deliver a presentation, I suggest you do the same.

## When *Not* to Look Them in the Eye

Eye contact is a powerful tool when handling a tough question. Too often I see speakers focus on a difficult questioner for far too long. People who hog the conversation like the spotlight, and you can move the spotlight from them by shifting your eye contact.

### Move It!

Have you ever listened to a press conference on the radio? Other than the speaker's voice, the sound you hear is that of cameras snapping wildly whenever the speaker moves. When a speaker raises an arm, cocks his head, clasps his hands, or walks away from the podium, he recaptures audience attention. Moving naturally—not mechanically—moves the needle.

Before we get to gestures, I want to address the importance of walking away from the podium—or from the head of the conference table. When you speak, it feels like there is an invisible barrier separating you from the audience. You break the barrier by moving away from your expected position. In so doing you wake up your listeners, connect better, and appear more confident. Try taking a few steps toward your audience when you are opening your remarks or delivering your call to action. But a word of caution: I have had powerful women tell me that in an audience dominated by men they feel they are perceived as overly aggressive when they do this. I have had tall men tell me they fear they are threatening when they approach listeners. So you should size up your audience when choreographing your moves. In general, I encourage a three-position physical presentation model to go along with the message points and proofs modules.

1. Position 1 is your home base (behind the podium, or standing at the head of the table). From this position, you make each of your message points.
2. Position 2 is a "step aside." Use this position to deliver your anecdotes (step aside for the aside). When you say, "let me

give you an example" or "let me tell you a little story" and then step aside, it looks as if something just came to you.

3. Position 3 is a move to an alternative visual medium—a flip chart or a video monitor. When you are using a visual to demonstrate a fact, you can quite naturally move to where the image is generated.

In everyday life we tend to move as we speak. The reason we don't do so when we speak formally is that we are nervous and feel frozen in place. With movement as with words, rehearsal is the key to appearing unrehearsed. Mark your text to indicate when you should move and practice those movements each time you practice your presentation.

I had a client who had a well-structured presentation to deliver, but she was very anxious and tended to grab onto the podium. The presentation started with a humorous story about the way hotel marketing used to be done. She then detailed the business environment today and concluded with a brief summary of the strategy that she explained in a PowerPoint. After she said her hello from the podium (Position 1), I got her to take three steps to the side of the podium (Position 2) to share her historical anecdote. She then moved to a video screen (Position 3) for a 30-second video clip that introduced her business strategy. Then she returned to Position 1 to begin her PowerPoint. Moving helped her change moods and kept the audience's attention. Throughout her presentation she would move to Position 2 for anecdotes and Position 3 for video clips. The changes also helped to keep her more relaxed.

### Gestures: The Right Kind in the Right Amount

We all naturally gesture in the course of conversation, so using gestures when you are in the spotlight can make you look and feel more comfortable and help you sound conversational. But don't try too hard. The only thing worse than no gestures is too many. You want to be you. In my training sessions I often tape people talking when they are not aware that the camera is on so they can see what gestures come naturally to them.

I work with gesture issues every day. Some people don't gesture enough and appear wooden. Some use inappropriate or repetitive gestures. And other people are in overdrive, gesturing all over

## Doing What Comes Naturally

Researchers at Emory University are studying how language evolved by observing the way that apes use gestures. They watched hundreds of hours of videotape in which chimps and bonobos—two separate species of apes that are humans' closest genetic relatives—used more than 30 distinct gestures like waving a hand, raising an arm, dabbing with a finger, and reaching out. The researchers linked each gesture to the context of what was going on at the moment. Language researcher Susan Goldin-Meadow from the University of Chicago finds this variety of gesturing intriguing and suggests that gestural communication may be a precursor to human language. Indeed, human infants gesture long before they speak, and "baby signing" is catching on, with parents learning to communicate with babies as young as a few months of age by using hand signs.

the place. One top executive I worked with was an experienced speaker who, one-on-one, came off as smart, amusing, and confident. But when he spoke to a group, he punctuated every sentence with the same chopping hand motion (remember the Tin Man in *The Wizard of Oz*?). He rendered what could be a strong gesture if used sparingly into one that was meaningless at best and, at worst, irritating. When I told my client this, he confided in despair that he didn't know what to do with his hands; I suggested he loosely fold his hands with his finger tips meeting, a gesture that is known as "steepling." I added that he could put at least one hand in his pocket just before he made a big point—at which time he would have license to chop.

Some people fail to gesture because they are in lockdown mode. They grip the podium for dear life, or clench their hands in front or behind their backs. The latter position is truly a throwback. For years, presentation coaches actually taught people to put their hands behind their backs in what is sometimes called the "Prince Charles stance." Since he's a prince, the thinking went, and *he* stands that way, it must be powerful. As it turns out, research shows most people find the gesture implies untrustworthiness. If we can't see what your hands are doing, we're a bit suspicious.

But beware of coaching that advises you to just let go of that podium. I remember the Democratic National Convention when

John Kerry got the Democrats' presidential nod. His acceptance speech was excellent, but only if you closed your eyes. That night, an emergency popped up and I had to be on the road for hours, so I listened to Kerry on the radio before I looked at the videotape. He sounded fine, but when I saw the tape I had another impression altogether. Kerry, like many politicians and executives who have been coached, had obviously been advised to let loose of the podium and "use your hands." Well, the Massachusetts senator looked like a Boston Pops conductor. Virtually every line was accompanied by a different set of gestures, and they were not always in concert with his words.

Kerry taught all of us some lessons that night. First, once you've decided where you want to use gestures in your talk, underline your text and practice them. You don't want to get caught pointing "me" when you mean "you" (if you do, the only real point you'll make is that you needed more practice). Next, be sure that your gestures fit the room size. Small, contained gestures can work with a small group; larger, more effusive ones are needed to speak to a big crowd. But be careful not to make your gestures too broad if you are being televised or they won't "fit" into people's living rooms (no, not even with those big flat panel TVs.).

That same night, Bill Clinton got up and delivered his messages in three-point mode. He used gestures extremely well, gesturing on the big takeaway points. For instance: With hands on the podium (not clutching the podium), Clinton declared in an earnest, firm, matter-of-fact manner, "We all honor the sacrifice of our men and women in uniform." (Pause.) "We all want good jobs, good schools, safe streets, a clean environment." (Pause.) Then, lowering his voice slightly and folding his hands loosely, he continued wistfully, "We all want our children to grow up in a secure America."(Pause.) Then he increased his volume, slowed his pace and said, "Our *DIFFERENCES* (as he stressed this key word he gestured) are how we want to *ACHIEVE* (same volume and gesture combination) these things." Clinton knows that gestures should be used for emphasis, to move the needle. He knows, too, that gestures can be used in concert with volume and speed to make strong points.

## "V" #2: Vocal Elements

Voice is the delivery vehicle for words. The way you use voice can be a powerful motivator. It can bring listeners under your spell.

But even the best words said in an inaudible or monotonous voice will fall short of their goal. In this section we'll look at volume, pacing, tone, and pitch: all critical elements of voice.

### Volume: The Art of Ups and Downs

Notice that in the foregoing example, Bill Clinton selected key words to stress. Before and after these words he actually *lowered* his voice. What does he know that many speakers do not? He knows that dropping your voice to nearly a whisper can be as effective as raising your voice. Lowering your voice tends to get the audience to lean in and listen carefully.

Effective speakers also recognize the need for variety in the softness and loudness of their voices. Of course it's important that everyone in the room hears you, and you can check at the beginning of your talk to make sure you are audible. (It's disconcerting to have people shout out, "Can't hear you," and even worse if they're afraid to say they can't hear and just tune out.) That said, however, it's important to avoid the temptation to start out too loudly. If you do, you will leave yourself nowhere to go.

### Pacing: Don't Race, Don't Dawdle

How quickly do you speak in front of an audience? For a lot of speakers, especially those who just-want to-get-it-over-with-already, the answer is: too fast. People talk at an average of 125 to 225 words per minute, but at the upper end of this range listeners stop listening. It's too much work. That FedEx fast-talker is funny, but we don't want to get our information that way.

On the other hand, speaking too slowly throughout your talk can also hurt your cause. In most situations, listeners will find a speaker with a somewhat faster rate than average to be more competent and persuasive. And although Hollywood and Broadway may stereotype fast-talkers as liars and con artists (from Professor Hill in *The Music Man* to "the great and powerful Oz"), research shows that slower speaking laced with stalling interjections ("err," "umm," "ahhh") is a more reliable indicator of lying.

So, what's the right pace? Fast or slow? The answer is: neither. Once again, variety is key as shown in the Bill Clinton example. In general, you should open your presentation slowly. It will help your audience absorb what you intend to tell them and help you relax a bit. You can pick up your pace to explain or prove your main points, but pause between them to let your information sink in and to add drama to your next point. You should also pause and slow a bit for your *summary* and your *call to action* modules. When working with speedy speakers (and I am a recovering one myself), I have them practice slowing down, but employing pauses is also effective and far easier to master. Glance down briefly at your notes or practice pausing as you switch slides. Just don't be afraid of the sound of silence. Used this way, silence is your ally.

## Fast Facts Are Like Fast Food

A human resources executive was presenting to leadership and addressing one of the company's greatest HR challenges: attracting and promoting a great and diverse workforce that looked like the customers the company wanted to sell to. She had 10 slides filled with all kinds of graphs and statistics, and she was speed-reading her way through all of them. She told me she had to present within her allotted time slot and thought a fact barrage was the best way to show her progress. But to really make her points, she needed to slow down and add an anecdote. Businesses like to measure success but she had turned a people story into strictly a numbers story—and her breakneck pace was making her fast facts like fast food—filling but ultimately unsatisfying and unremarkable. Adding an anecdote about an exceptional and very satisfied employee allowed her to vary her pace along with her proofs.

### Tone and Pitch: Emotional Cues and Clues

Did your mom or dad ever say to you, "Don't use that tone with me!" Your words may have been "Sure, Mom, I'd be happy to do the dishes," but your tone told her otherwise. It doesn't matter what words were spoken if the tone, (i.e., the sound quality of your voice) said something different. Tone and pitch—pitch being the highness or lowness of voice inflection—provide an additional track of information to listeners. They tell what you really think about what you are saying, and, more generally, how you feel about yourself. That in turn affects how your message is received and what the audience thinks of you.

There have been a number of studies on pitch and persuasion, and all suggest that a speaker with a higher pitched voice is seen as less truthful and less persuasive. Such speakers are viewed as weaker and more nervous, which, by the way, is often the reason for the higher pitch. I recently worked with a client who confidently got up and set the stage for her upcoming presentation, but the minute she began to rehearse, her pitch jumped up an octave. She sounded nervous and less authoritative than she did just seconds before in front of the same group of colleagues. Recognizing the difference on tape, the next time up she made a conscious effort to lower her voice. She wasn't less nervous, but she was far more persuasive. Clients often comment on my voice as sounding authoritative. Only part is what genetics gave me, the lions share is what NBC gave me by training me to use the lower range of my voice. Over time it became natural. It will for you. Just don't go overboard. The key is to sound natural, not like Ted Baxter the pompous anchorman with the booming voice on the old *Mary Tyler Moore Show*.

Like pitch, tone affects your credibility, whether or not listeners like what they hear and whether or not they believe and accept it. Tone can have an immense impact on listeners' emotional reactions. For example, a Harvard study found that surgeons who spoke to patients in a dominating and indifferent tone were more likely to be sued for malpractice than those whose tone signaled concern. Just a few seconds of listening to a surgeon's tone of voice was enough for researchers to accurately predict which physicians would unwittingly invite litigation.

Fortunately, most of us won't get sued over our tone of voice, but tone does tend to give us problems when we speak. In our everyday lives, most of us use quite a variety of tone and pitch. Yet in many cases, as speakers in front of an audience, we say everything in one monotonous tone.

I once noticed a client was speaking in a monotone while introducing leading scientists at an industry conference. He viewed his speech as a block of text to be gotten through with big word land mines he didn't want to stumble over. His introductions fell naturally into three distinct parts: a bit of awe-inspiring science history ("Did you know that . . . ?"), an link between an historical and a current trends, and a short bio for each scientist establishing each as a leader in the trend. I asked the speaker what tone he would use if he were describing an incredible scientific discovery to his high school-age son and he said, "wonderment." We had our tone for his opening segments. For his second segments he talked about current trends in a more grounded, authoritative tone (moving to the side of the podium as he did so), and for the final segments of short bios he switched to a brisk, housekeeping tone (moving to a video screen that added a visual element to the introductions). It was a 100 percent improvement.

Notice that this speaker did not simply vary his tone arbitrarily. Rather, he was careful to match his tone to the content in a way that made emotional sense. When researchers at Stanford University studied tone of voice they found, not surprisingly, that people report liking content more when emotion and content match.

Common sense says that if you have happy news to impart, listeners expect your tone to be happy, to convey energy, melody, and bounce. If you have somber news they expect your words to be spoken at a lower pitch in a serious tone and to convey less energy. There is, however, one situation when you should, in fact, shift to neutral in terms of your voice tone. Those same Stanford studies found that a neutral tone of voice actually adds to your credibility when you are delivering information that is controversial and you already have a skeptical audience. This, too, makes sense when you think about it. Because tone of voice is so emotionally influential, your neutrality may influence an audience whose "mind is made up" into taking an objective look at new information.

### Even Billionaires Watch Their Tone

When Bill Gates was getting ready to deliver his commencement speech to Harvard's class of 2007, he carefully worked on his message calling on students to become active in solving global inequities. He was concerned, however, about delivering such a message in the right tone. He sought help on delivery and tone from fellow billionaire Warren Buffett. According to the *Wall Street Journal,* Gates said after his meeting with Buffett, "Warren helped me feel like really telling the students to do something was okay if you did it the right way."

## "V" #3: Verbal Elements

In this section we'll look at your words and how you choose them. Although I've devoted a lot of this chapter to visuals and vocal style, I don't want to leave you with the impression that words are in any way less important. The Mehrabian study I cited earlier is often misinterpreted in such a way. Remember, Mehrabian's primary finding was that people give less credence to words when the visual and vocal signs that accompany them are incongruent. The point is that you want all your ducks in a row when you present: You want your visual and vocal style to reinforce rather than detract from or contradict the very important words you want to say.

That being the case, when it comes to words, one of the main things speakers need to consider is authenticity. You could be the most honest person in the world, speaking the most truthful words, and still be disbelieved if you fail to choose words that convey your genuine intent.

### Avoid Lockstep Rhetoric

If you've ever watched Sunday morning political talk shows, or the recaps of them that routinely appear on Comedy Central's *Daily Show,* you're aware that politicians, cabinet members, and White House officials often utter the same rehearsed sound bytes over and over again. They speak the same words—words that appear to have been "focus grouped" within an inch of their lives—in response to almost any question, whether they seem to answer that question or not.

If you watch business shows on CNBC, Bloomberg Television, or the like, you often see executives and corporate spokespersons doing exactly the same thing. In lockstep with everyone else in their organization they are mouthing the same messages, word for word. In fact, the more controversial the situation—a product recall, an SEC investigation—the less likelihood that anyone will diverge from what everyone whose television-viewing has progressed beyond *Teletubbies* can recognize as a script.

But in politics or business the effect is the same: Lockstep rhetoric comes off as evasive. This is not to say the words themselves are not truthful. They may be accurate, but they *sound* suspect.

Absolutely, it is important for an organization's members to be aligned in the messages they want to convey. But that need not mean speaking like automatons. Organizations don't do themselves any favors when they try to micromanage speech. It's best to urge employees to stay on message while using words and phrases that come naturally to them.

### Call a Spade a Spade

Along the same lines, I've noticed a trend in certain fields where certain words—perfectly good words that all listeners seem to understand—are boycotted. Usually this is because those words are thought to conjure up some undesirable connotations. (That is why, I presume, the U.S. Department of Agriculture no longer refers to "hunger," but rather to "very low food security.") But such word boycotts tend to go too far. The deliberate omission comes off as silly at best. At worst it inspires cynicism, the result being that the avoided word is the one all listeners are thinking even though no one is saying it aloud.

I'm reminded of a hotel chain that was offering what amounted to a slightly modified—and very upscale—version of a time-share arrangement. Its representatives struggled mightily to describe the new offering while steadfastly avoiding, or at least trying to avoid, the dreaded "t-s" word. But the fact was that there was no other easily understood word to describe the product. I watched as employee after employee stumbled. "It's like a t—, uh, it's, you know, a sharing arrangement, well, not exactly sharing, um . . ." All they had to do was say "upscale time-share" and everyone would have gotten it. As it was, listeners felt confused and a little suspicious.

The bottom line: Don't substitute a euphemism or a contrived highfalutin synonym when you have a perfectly good word at hand. And never use three or four words when one will do. Listeners don't like having to guess at what you're saying, and chances are most of them left their secret decoder rings at home. Call a spade a spade and a time-share a time-share and you won't waste anyone's precious time, least of all your own.

### The Cool Rule

Finally, here's a rule that anyone with teenaged children is sure to understand right away: Don't use words that are not a normal part of your vocabulary in an attempt to appear "cool" or to be perceived as younger than you are. If you do, you will incite in your audience the same eye-rolling, headshaking pity that you incite in your sons and daughters when you do the same. Granted, your audience might not sigh as loudly in response to your egregious verbal gaffe as your children do, and they probably won't skulk off into a corner and pretend not to know you. But underneath their polite veneer they will be embarrassed for you.

Besides, if you are any older than a high school senior you just can't win when you use slang of any kind. It all changes too quickly, and yesterday's trendy words can mark you as a dinosaur today.

As with the other verbal caveats mentioned here, the point of this one is to get you to be yourself. The more "you" you can put into your words, and the more extraneous influences you can avoid, the better off you will be. For being yourself is, when all is said and done, the essence of what style is all about.

## Variety: The Spice of Speaking

Finally, there a fourth "V" I want you to keep in mind: Variety. There's a reason why variety is known as the spice of life. Without it, anything is bland. Every entertainer, every writer, every musician, every news producer knows this. Although you should introduce stylistic elements in your speech to relieve monotony and boredom, be sure not to overdo any one of them. The biggest problem I see with speakers doing something for emphasis is that they do it too often. It amounts to boldfacing **every word** in your Word document. The device, whatever it is, loses its impact and becomes annoying besides.

Imagine an audiometer, one of those panels on sound systems that register a jump with a change in volume. Speakers who move people "move the needle." But great speakers vary more than how loudly they speak. They also vary their body movements their facial expressions, their hand gestures, the pace and tone of their voice, and their choice of words.

The bottom line: Mix it up. In a way, speaking is like romance. Sameness is dull. Predictability is boring. Even the most polished style in the world will wear thin after a while if there are no surprises.

If you are preparing for a big presentation, have colleagues or family members give you feedback. You can download a presentation evaluation form that I use with my clients from my web site: www.civiello.com.

## Top Tips

1. Style is the presentation lie detector—ensure your credibility by making sure your visual, vocal, and verbal cues are consistent with your message.
2. Your body and your voice are important presentation tools, but don't neglect the importance of choosing words that convey authenticity rather than conformity.
3. Variety moves the needle . . . vary what you do and what you say to keep the audience engaged.

# Time Sense

## THE LINCOLN LEGACY

Ask any American to quote from a speech—any speech—and chances are they'll start out, "Fourscore and seven years ago . . ." In the Gettysburg Address, one of the most renowned presentations in history, Abraham Lincoln eloquently redefined the Civil War not as a struggle between North and South but as a "new birth of freedom" that would bring about the equality the Founding Fathers espoused. You probably know that the Gettysburg Address was short, but perhaps you don't know how short. It was, in fact, 10 sentences: 272 words. It took two minutes to deliver.

Another thing that many people don't know is that it was another speaker—Harvard President William Everett—who, on that day in 1863, should have delivered the definitive oratory dedicating the battlefield as a cemetery. Everett's speech was actually the one featured on the front pages of the newspapers the following day, with Lincoln's relegated to the inside pages. But only one speech became immortal.

Are you wondering why we don't recall that *other* Gettysburg address? Perhaps because it lasted *two hours* and began:

> Standing beneath this serene sky, overlooking these broad fields now reposing from the labors of the waning year, the mighty Alleghenies dimly towering before us, the graves of our brethren beneath our feet, it is with hesitation that I raise my poor voice to break the eloquent silence of God and Nature . . .

I'm guessing that was a long two hours.

But while it's easy enough for us to extol the brilliance behind Lincoln's brevity, most of us seem not to practice what we preach; rather we just preach and preach and preach *ad infinitum*. It's amazing how many of us ramble on before—and after—making our salient points. Yet the dilemma is understandable. Sometimes it's hard to know when to quit, especially if we've never consciously thought about developing what I call *time sense*—that is, an awareness of and respect for the realistic attention capacity of your audience.

The art of developing time sense is the subject of this chapter.

## Our Patience Is Thinning

Developing time sense is critical, especially today. The difference between yesteryear and this year is that today almost no one would sit through Everett's extended soliloquy—at least not willingly. A public figure whom I recall preached for two hours (well, one hour, 55 minutes and 27 seconds to be exact) was Fidel Castro when he addressed the United Nations in 1960—in an era when his country had missiles pointed at the United States—and so commanded lots of (grudging) attention.

For better or worse, we are a society whose patience grows more abbreviated with each passing year.

When I started as a television news reporter in 1976, the average sound bite was 30 to 40 seconds and the average story 1 minute 45 seconds to 2 minutes. Today the average story runs 1 minute 15 seconds. The average sound bite today is 10 seconds, and 2- to 5-second sound bites and blasts of natural sound (a horn honking or a door slamming or someone shouting, "I'm not going to take it anymore!") are used to pace each piece.

### If Elected, I'll . . .

One study of attention span says our interest and focus typically start to flag after as little as nine seconds.

If anyone must respond to this reality it is presidential candidates. According to Daniel Hallin in his book *We Keep America on Top of the World,* candidates during the 1968 election were allotted an average sound bite length of 43.1 seconds by the media. Twenty years later, the 1988 candidates were allotted 8.9 seconds. By my observation, the 2008 candidates have their words parsed in even smaller increments—sometimes five seconds or less.

By the late 1990s, we had a zealous assistant news director at my station who would watch that TRT—total running time—like a hawk. *Nothing* ran more than 1 minute 15 seconds unless you got special permission. Of course, big stories could be an exception then, and the same goes today. If a reporter nails an interview with the Iranian leader or a mass murderer or, yes, Paris Hilton talking for the first time about her stint in the slammer, news management might let them exceed the limit and may even devote a special show to the scoop. But remember, even that show will be broken up with advertisements every seven minutes or so. And on either side of those commercials will be summaries to keep people awake, or to bring them up to speed if they drifted off or moved away from the tube for a minute.

News management measures audience slip off, that is, the number of viewers who stop watching a broadcast. Every morning, as a news anchor for *Today in New York,* I was handed a Nielsen report that captured audience strength minute to minute. In today's environment, business presenters need to pay the same level of attention to audience attention. Presentations, like newscasts, need to be choreographed—beginning, middle, and end—to attract and maintain listeners.

In order to do this you'll need to do three things:

1. Cut to the chase (open).
2. Jolt so they don't bolt (middle).
3. Time your modules to allow adjustment (end).

## Cut to the Chase

A listener's attention is often highest at the start of your talk or presentation, so it is really important that you cut to the chase in the beginning of your presentation. One way you can do that is through your headline, which was discussed in Chapter 5. Whatever you do, don't bury that headline or dawdle along the path to it. Be aware that time is of the essence. And above all, remember this: *People rarely will sit still for something they didn't sit down for.*

Let me tell you what I mean. A few years ago, I attended a luncheon where the speaker opened by ringing some meditation chimes and asking her audience—a pack of hard-driving New York media and publishing types—to engage in three minutes of silence while breathing deeply. This, she said, would make us more receptive to her message.

This was not the opening of a speech by a yoga teacher or a stress management expert or the Dalai Lama. The speaker was someone who had played a significant part in New York's history—the Central Park jogger. Fourteen years after her brutal assault she had gone public with her identity and a message urging support of friends and strangers in need.

Years before, NBC had assigned me to cover the trial of this woman's accused assailants gavel to gavel. Listening to her on that day, I applauded her resilience and her courage. To a lesser extent, I even applauded her attempt to open a speech a little bit differently. But it just didn't work. First, a solitary meditation—something one might do to relax and center oneself—did not feel aligned with her message of reaching out and connecting with others. Second, three minutes was far too long a time. Though everyone complied out of respect, people became fidgety and self-conscious. Thirdly, her opening really did not suit her audience—busy writers, editors, and publishers who typically have ants in their pants. Sitting in silence for several minutes was not what busy people wanted to do in the middle of the day; they wanted to hear how the speaker had overcome her trauma.

The speaker could have done some brief variation on her unorthodox opening, perhaps using the bells to demonstrate focus on what is truly important in life—that might have been more appropriate. But as it was, she lost and confused a number of people, and even those who stayed with her felt a little manipulated. None of us had anything against meditation *per se*—it just wasn't what we came for.

Recently a friend of mine told me another story that exemplified the problem of not cutting to the chase. She was at her gym, where the management was trying to get members to sign up for a new exercise class. They were showing a video to entice people. My friend, on her way to another class, was mildly interested. She said sure, she'd sit and watch for a second. The video began with this pronouncement: "From time to time, the world is changed by a great revolution." Uh-oh. Sure enough, the next minute was devoted to a montage of Paul Revere, Bastille Day, Thomas Edison and the light bulb, the Wright Brothers at Kitty Hawk, and so on. All my friend wanted was to see what the exercise routines looked like to get a sense of whether the new class was something she wanted to try. She was really irritated. She didn't have a minute, or even a few seconds, for something so irrelevant.

When you linger, loiter, or go round and round on your way to your main message, you're in danger of not only boring people but also alienating them. The message you're inadvertently sending is that their time isn't valuable. But to each of us, our time is a priceless commodity. Once gone, we can't wish it back or buy it back. Think about how you feel when someone else squanders your time—the guy in the "10 items" line who has 14 items (and coupons!), the customer service phone rep who consigns you to Musak limbo, the cable repairman who says he'll be there between 8:00 and 12:00 (and shows up at 3:00). Now try that shoe on the other foot and imagine being the guilty party. Do you think anyone will harbor warm feelings for you? Remember a golden rule of presentation: **Don't waste for others what you wouldn't waste for yourself.**

### Spit It Out

*The Journal of the American Medical Association* says the average patient visiting a doctor in the United States gets 23 seconds to make an initial statement before the conversation is redirected by the doctor. Ironically, most patients conclude their statements in 29 seconds if allowed to finish. But that six-second gap isn't likely to go away. Making your point during the beginning of your consultation with your doctor could conceivably make the difference between life and death. Just like making your point at the start of your presentation can make the difference between whether your speech will fly or die.

## Jolt So They Don't Bolt

The second thing you need to do in order to attract and maintain listeners is jolt in the middle of the speech so your audience doesn't bolt. This revelation is what my clients are finding most helpful. Understand that attention is high at the beginning of a speech. It's also high at the end of a speech—when audience members are listening for your summary because they have drifted off in the middle. This drifting off in the middle phenomenon, that we talked about in Chapter 1, is so common that speakers almost take it for granted. It's as if we fully expect to stuff our audience into a bottle and toss them out to sea midway through our presentation, and then wait for the tide to bring them back in.

But why do that to them, not to mention to yourself? Look at it this way: They've already shown up; you've already shown up. It would be foolish not to make the most of the time you've all committed.

To keep your audience from drifting off in the middle, you need to jolt them, in other words reopen partway through your talk. This means doing or saying something that significantly changes the look or pace of your presentation. It could be:

- Introducing a video.
- Polling the audience.
- Enlisting another speaker for a cameo appearance.
- Simply moving from a podium to a flip chart.
- Using a picture vs. a graph in your PowerPoint.

In the course of a typical 20-minute presentation, you should plan on re-opening, or jolting, about every 7 minutes at the very least. This works perfectly with presentations structured around three message points. Remember the Jolt So They Don't Bolt graph in Chapter 1? (See Figure 7.1.)

This is precisely the theory behind the 30-minute newscast, which actually has 22 minutes of context after you subtract the time for commercials. Each newscast has two seven- or eight-minute modules called "news blocks" followed by a two- to three-minute weather and sports block, ending with a one- to two-minute news summary, maybe a feature story, and goodnight.

In newscasts, the jolt is accomplished by methods of substance and style, that is, what is said and how it's said.

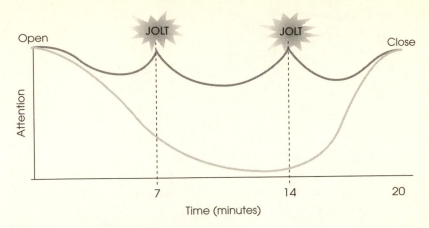

**Figure 7.1    Listening Curve and Cure**

**Visually:** The anchor will turn to another camera and inform viewers what is coming up next.

**Vocally:** The anchor's tone will change (for example, from a somber tone for a serious story to a brighter tone for a lighter piece.

**Verbally:** The anchor will tease what's in store for the viewer. For example, there might be a two-second clip of a politician shouting, "I'll fight." And the anchor will say, "We'll see what has the senator fightin' mad when we come back."

The important thing is that you do *something* different in the midst of your talk. You should plan ahead for it, and insert "jolt notes" to yourself in your presentation. But you should also be alert to whether audience attention is fading at times other than those when your jolts are preplanned. If so, try one of these techniques for an instant jolt:

**Ask a question.** Do not ask just any random question (don't simply stop and ask if anyone knows the capital of Idaho). Look at your next slide or find your next fact and turn that into a question. Ask if anyone has experience with the information you are about to deliver.

**Call on someone.** Calling on someone works well in any situation, and is also one of the few jolts you can use if you are taking the lead in speaking during a conference call. I have a client who has to present to several hundred people on such calls and she is just never sure, no matter how well her presentation seems to be going, how many people are listening versus how many people are writing e-mails or downloading music from iTunes. We decided it would be a good idea for her to call on people but, as she didn't want to put anyone on the spot I, suggested she warn a few participants ahead of time. Her calling on *some* people put everyone else on notice that they might be called on as well.

Of course you can feel free to improvise your own jolting techniques, or to mix and match any mentioned here. Play with jolts as you rehearse. Vary your movement and tone. Use your words to tease "coming attractions." Ask questions. Call in reinforcements. Insert video clips or other visual aids. Go for a laugh if it's appropriate. The important thing is to be alert to when your audience is drifting. Then throw them a lifeline and reel them back in.

### Time for a Jolt? Decoding Audience Body Language

Is it time to jolt? The body language of your audience will give you some clues.

*Eyes cast downward:* They're peeking at their Blackberries.

*Eyes cast upward:* They're thinking of what they have to do later or petitioning heaven for you to keep it short.

*Eyes on your face:* You've got them hooked.

*Eyes on your clothes:* Your clothes are more interesting than you are. (This is not good unless you're Paris Hilton.)

*Slouching posture:* They're dozing, or text messaging.

*Upright posture:* They're all yours.

*Smiling when you're not being funny:* They're in their own world, or their cell phone is vibrating in an erogenous zone.

## Time Your Modules, Adjust as Needed

Figuring how to control your time is a step most people rarely take in their presentation preparation. As we touched on in Chapter 1, you need to time your presentation, module by module, map it out, and have a Plan B.

In a basic 20-minute presentation, the most common time frame in the business world, modules should take approximately the following lengths of time:

| | |
|---|---:|
| Headline | 1 minute |
| Context | 1 minute |
| Message Point 1 (with proofs) | 5 minutes |
| Message Point 2 (with proofs) | 5 minutes |
| Message Point 3 (with proofs) | 5 minutes |
| Summary | 1 minute |
| Call to Action | 2 minutes |

Note that I've left out signposts in the count because these refrains typically take only seconds.

Note also that each message point includes the proofs—in the form of facts, anecdotes, and analogies—that support it. It's a good idea to vary the lengths of these proofs from point to point to keep things interesting.

Mapping out your modules serves multiple purposes. First, it lets you know right off the bat whether your presentation fits the time that's been allotted to you. Second, it lets you know if you're lopsided, if you're devoting too much time to any one point while giving short shrift to others. Third, and this is extremely important, it lets you see where you can trim your presentation if circumstances change.

For example, I was working with an internal communications team at a pharmaceutical company. They were preparing a 20-minute presentation for their CEO about what they'd accomplished and what they planned to do in the coming year.

Their headline was, "We've done a great job to improve relations with the media, including our work with the speaker's bureau, and now we plan to get great mileage out of your pet project—a NASCAR sponsorship that will promote our new blood pressure medicine." Their context was focused on how they linked up with the speaker's bureau and what it had accomplished. They wanted to make three points:

1. They'd done a good job with a speaker's bureau program that they no longer ran.
2. They'd improved the company web site and wanted approval for additional steps.
3. They had a strong publicity program lined up for a sporting event they were sponsoring.

But they told me that their CEO had a short attention span and a reputation for slashing presenters' time or for interrupting so much that speakers never got to make all of their points. So we planned and practiced cutting the presentation in half, as you'll see in their time sense roadmap in Figure 7.2. Specifically, they did the following:

- They decided message point 1 could be reduced to a minute. After all, they no longer ran the program (it had been given to human resources), and the CEO did not much care about yesterday. They decided they would provide only one proof for this point: the fact that the head of sales estimated the speaker program increased leads by 50 percent.
- They eliminated the context module.
- They eliminated message point 2. The web site improvements could be addressed at another time. Instead they planned to use the web site as an anecdotal proof for message point 3— that they were using the web site to drum up publicity for the NASCAR event.
- They left intact message point 3, their highest priority and a sweet spot for the boss, who was a big NASCAR fan. The idea behind the sponsorship was that they would set up a tent and test blood pressure for NASCAR fans—who would not only find out their blood pressure, but also learn about the drug company's new medication.

After summing up, the team asked for the CEO's support to increase the budget for the web site, which would be used to get people and the press to visit the tent.

| Module | Time Plan A | Time Plan B |
|---|---|---|
| **Headline** | 1.0 | 1.0 |
| **Context** | 1.0 | x |
| **Point 1 (People)** | | |
| Fact | 1.0 | 1.0 |
| Anecdote | 2.0 | x |
| Analogy | 2.0 | x |
| **Point 2 (Product)** | | |
| Fact | 1.0 | x |
| Anecdote | 2.0 | x |
| Analogy | 2.0 | x |
| **Point 3 (Price)** | | |
| Fact | 1.0 | 1.0 |
| Anecdote | 2.0 | 2.0 |
| Analogy | 2.0 | 2.0 |
| **Signpost & Summary** | 1.0 | 1.0 |
| **Call to Action** | 2.0 | 2.0 |
| **Total Time** (in minutes) | 20.0 | 10.0 |

**Figure 7.2   Time Your Modules**

By flexing the time of their modules, this team took complete control of the brief time they had to make their case with an impatient CEO. You can take similar command, in any situation, and avoid getting your message amputated.

Until now, you might have reacted to a shortened presentation time as most people do: by trying to cram in too much information and by talking too fast. But the result of such tactics is that everything you say comes out sounding like gibberish. You end up getting nothing across instead of highlighting the most important information. Don't race; keep your pace, but make sure you are using every moment of your precious time wisely.

## Too Many Words?

The average speech rate in the mid-Atlantic states is 120 to 140 words a minute. It's faster in some places, like New York City, and slower in others. But if you speak at a rate of about 125 words a minute, it's a pretty safe bet that listeners will keep up.

How can you gauge? One double-spaced typewritten page is approximately 250 words. If you are getting through that page in about two minutes, you're on track.

As for slides, in general, you should keep a slide on screen for about a minute, though you might vary this depending on the complexity of its content.

## Overtime Is a Crime

Now that we've talked about shortening a presentation, you might be wondering if there's ever a reason to go over your time. In general, the rule is: no. *It's a crime to go over your time.*

Of course, as with all rules, there is the occasional exception. If someone else is running late or is a no-show and you need to fill time in an agenda, or if you are addressing a very small audience where you can tell people are extremely interested and want more information, all is forgiven. In fact, it's always a good idea to have a few extra support modules at the ready should such circumstances arise.

For the most part, however, there are few business-oriented messages that cannot be adequately conveyed in the course of 20 minutes.

(The same can be said of most messages of any kind. To quote the famous slogan of New York City's all-news-all-the-time radio station, WINS: "You give us 22 minutes; we'll give you the world!") Besides, assuming you're not going to be abducted by a spaceship once your presentation is done, people know where to find you if they want to know more.

Think of it this way: When you begin your talk, the audience is hungry for information, and you should quickly give them something to chew on. Partway through their meal, they want their palette piqued by a fresh new course; that's when you should jolt their appetites. But when they come to the end of everything you've served, they should feel full and satisfied. There's no reason to overfeed them. They'll leave bloated and groggy if you do.

---

**Top Tips**

1. Time your modules, not just your total speech time, so you can adjust your talk more easily, and remember a 20-minute presentation is long enough.
2. Jolt so they don't bolt—poll, ask a question, use a flip chart; do something different to reel them back in.
3. Cut to the chase as soon as possible, no matter how long you have to speak.

# PART

# III

# PRESENTATION SITUATIONS

# Hold That Elevator

## THE ONE-MINUTE MESSAGE

"You wait just one minute young fella."

"Wait a minute . . . I've got an idea!"

"Give me a minute. I'll be right with you."

Ah, the poor, maligned minute. One minute has always seemed like the briefest of pauses, like nothing at all. In fact, a minute— 60 seconds brimming with potential—is probably the most misunderstood unit of time.

Just start an egg timer or a microwave timer, or look at any digital clock in the room right now and start talking out loud for a minute. Say who you are, say what you do and why, and say just one way that you do it better than anyone else. I will bet that you will have time to spare!

In the TV news business, stories the anchor reads run, on average, 20 seconds. And those stories have to give the who, what, when and why in a way that makes viewers care. Full-blown news stories run only a little more than a minute. And that includes space for dueling sound bites: the frazzled town mayor versus the guy who thinks he should be allowed to put a zoo in his backyard.

The long and the short of it: a minute offers a lot of time and a lot of opportunity. In a minute:

- You can network.
- You can preview.
- You can promote.
- You can prosper.

When you have a precious minute, don't fritter it away. This chapter will show you how to make the most of a minute by using the modular method. The trick is to distill the essence of your message into a pithy and potent form.

## Be Ready with a Boilerplate

Many of the people whom we call lucky are really just those who are always ready to make the most of the moment. When opportunity knocks, they answer the door. That's why when you run into someone at a cocktail party, a trade show or in the elevator, or when you think you might get a minute of face time, you must be prepared. Even if you can't foresee any such circumstance happening, you should operate on the assumption that it could. Whatever your message is, you need to be ready to deliver it succinctly and memorably whenever an appropriate minute arises.

### Waste Not and They'll Want More

There's nothing worse than running into a potential customer/investor/employer, having them ask, "So, what do you do?" and you drop the ball. You talk too much about too little or you simply say too little, freezing up you squeak, "Oh I'm in consulting." Hmm. I bet that when they've moved on you'll be thinking, "Darn, if only I'd said such and such."

It's worth avoiding that awful "What the heck am I going to say?" moment by crafting an intriguing boilerplate. As Mark Twain once said, "I never could make a good impromptu speech without several hours to prepare it."

Whenever a client is preparing for a 20-, 30-, or 60-minute talk, I always urge him to start with one minute. Boil it down to a minute's worth of "concentrate" and you can always expand it. Think of your message like food that is flavorful and potent—like curry paste or pesto. You can always add water or broth to dilute an intense flavor, but its essence will remain and resonate.

Creating what I call "the elevator speech" is often perceived as quite a challenge. It is easier to ramble on than to be concise. But the payoff is worth the work. If you can pique interest in the time it takes for an elevator to travel from the ground floor to the top floor it can eventually help you get to the corner office.

Crafting a great elevator module begins, as all good message formulation does, with knowing who your audience is and what they want. Know what problem your potential listener cares most about and how you can help.

- If it is a potential customer: How can you help him do business better?
- If it is your boss: How can you help her get the job done so she looks good to her boss?
- If it is a reporter: What do you have to tell his readers or viewers that they don't already know?

With this in mind, you're ready to organize your one-minute elevator module. The structure is similar to that of a longer presentation, but streamlined:

| | |
|---|---|
| Open | Greeting and personal introduction (who are you?) if needed |
| Three Message Points | |
| Message Point 1 | What you are doing |
| Message Point 2 | Why you are doing it |
| Message Point 3 | Why you do it differently/better |
| Quick Proof | One fact, analogy, or anecdote |
| Call to Action | What you want them to do |

For some people I have worked with, the first message point, saying what they do, is a stumbling block. They describe their occupations or businesses so simply ("I'm a consultant") that it becomes meaningless. You need to be simple, yet specific.

Others can get hung up on the second message point—why they do what they do. In order to help people answer these questions, I ask: What do you do for people? What do you contribute? Why is the world a better place because you do what you do?

For many people, the toughest part seems to be the third message point: saying how what they do is different or better. If someone is, say, a financial advisor at a major brokerage house he might tell me, at first, that he essentially does what financial advisors at other major institutions do. That's the point at which I start asking about specifics. Are you given more independence as an advisor? Do you use a particular product, program or software that helps you be more responsive to your clients? Would your clients say you are very accessible? Ultimately, he will have an "Aha!" moment and realize his personal differentiators and consequently be able to describe why his services are different or better.

It's also a good idea if the quick proof you select supports your differentiator message point. Think of a fact, analogy, or anecdote (the latter is the most soft sell and best for casual encounters) that supports why you are better.

Finally, whatever you do, don't neglect the call to action. The ultimate goal of the one-minute module is to convey enough information to pique further interest. You won't get anyone to sign a contract or offer you a job in an elevator—but you can inform and intrigue them. What does success sound like? "So Ed, give me a call or drop me an e-mail and we'll talk some more." Yessss!

## "Got a Minute?" Keep It Conversational

Whether you have a minute or an hour, you still need to follow the principle that your style of speech is as important as what you say. In most brief encounters, especially in social settings or when the encounter is by chance, striking a conversational tone is your best bet. You don't want to come across as selling when the setting isn't conducive.

Practice modifying your elevator module so that you'll be ready for any number of situations. For example, here's how Ed might approach a potential client he runs into at a trade show:

(*Open*) Hi, Ron. It's Ed Winston. We met at the public relations award banquet last year. It's good to see you again.

(*What you are doing?*) I've left Pearson PR and have started my own company, Winston Reed Communications, with another Pearson colleague. We specialize in high-tech businesses like yours.

(*Why?*) We can focus on exactly the kind of coverage you need—whether it's thought leadership opportunities, trade shows, or news coverage.

(*What's different?*) We really work in a targeted way. No throwing spaghetti at the wall and seeing what sticks.

(*Proof*) In fact, we just had one of our clients on the cover of *Wired.*

(*Call to action*) Would it be all right if I gave you a call?

Of course you don't want to do this machine gun style. You want to open up your message for some indication your audience is interested. For instance after your differentiator you'll want to hear a green light like, "Yes, I just got rid of a firm like that."

Ed could use the same message points when a venture capitalist calls him in for an update, but here a more bulleted business tone will work. It demonstrates that Ed has prepared and is ready to elaborate.

(*Open*) Morning, Dillon. Things are going very well.

(*What are you doing?*) Our strategy to specialize in high-tech business is a good one.

(*Why?*) High tech is really coming back and customizing public relations plans for each client is working.

(*What's different?*) We just got Zipper Net on the cover of *Wired* magazine! It's that kind of success that's winning us clients.

(*Proof*) In the last six months we have doubled our client base . . . roughly half on retainer for a year or more. And all this from word of mouth and no real marketing budget.

(*Call to action*) That said, we'd like to talk about a marketing campaign with you today.

One thing you definitely want to steer clear of in an elevator module is jargon. I once asked an executive from a telecommunications company to come up with a minute-long message. He described his company as "an integrated communications powerhouse leading the changing of the guard within the emerging new era of telecommunications."

That was supported by three points:

1. We are defining a new industry standard through our commitment to add assets, attract powerful partnerships, and deliver the world's most advanced communications products and services.

    (Do you know what they do yet?)

2. We have a strong balance sheet and a diversified revenue stream allowing us to emerge as the leading next-generation communications company.

    (Oh?)

3. We are the first to provide an all-optical, switched-based network uniquely positioned to anticipate and respond to tomorrow's communications landscape and demonstrate the true meaning of speed and accountability.

    (I still defy anyone to tell me what they do, let alone why.)

And that is what he "boiled down"! All I can say is that if I heard this at a cocktail party I would probably want to have several more cocktails.

---

### No Time to Be Negative

The U.S. Congress allows members one-minute speeches, three hundred words, before or after each legislative business day to discuss any topic they want if they follow the rules. They are specifically *not* allowed to call legislators names or label their actions as stupid. But you'd never know it. YouTube regularly features these little gems. An example: *"I want to state my absolute disgust about the unbelievably stupid vote yesterday in the Senate of the United States."* Whoops, that's a rule breaker and, more importantly, a waste of time. When you've only got a minute, use it. Be proactive. Promote your own agenda; don't denigrate someone else's. It's a waste of valuable time.

---

## Respecting Boundaries: Moments *Not* to Seize the Moment

I don't want to leave you with the impression that any time is the right time for a one-minute message. Seizing the moment is one thing, but being an insensitive boor is quite another. If you fail to respect social boundaries it doesn't matter what you say. The only message you'll send is that you don't know how to handle yourself appropriately.

I know a woman who is the admissions director of a very selective private preschool in Manhattan. She tells the story of how the mom of a would-be student approached her for an application for her "gifted" toddler as she was getting out of the shower at the gym. Quite obviously, the director did not have an application handy—and, more to the point, I'll bet she didn't send one to this over-eager parent. It wouldn't have mattered if the toddler in question were Mozart.

Then there's the president of an independent film company who gets hit up at every turn. Everyone has written a little screenplay they want to send his way. One day he was in a restaurant celebrating a new movie deal. The champagne was flowing. There were lots of people, his team, the stars . . . and a waiter who was pushing a script. The server leaned over to whisper the plot. The film boss's face fell. He said, "Listen man, I'm a little busy here, can you—" But the waiter pressed on. Needless to say, that was a screenplay that never got a reading.

In a similar vein, I was at a holiday party when a woman hit up the town's wealthiest and most generous person for funding for a new teen center. "We just need fifty thousand more," she said. Her problem was she was too direct, cutting straight to the call to action. Instead, she should have talked up the why of her cause (kids in town were bored and getting into trouble; they needed to have some supervised place to play videogames, do homework, and listen to music), offer a proof (I'd previously heard her tell an anecdote about the success of a similar center in a nearby town), and then lightly say, "We're almost there on the funding. I'll give you a call later." Only if the potential donor wanted more specific information then and there should she have offered it.

When I was a reporter, people would pitch stories to me at the worst times and places. One time I was in the grocery store with my two toddlers—one squirming and whining in the cart and wanted out and the other intent on rearranging the jam and jelly shelves—when a complete stranger approached, said she watched me every morning, and began to tell me how she had evidence that a major New York department store was selling winter boots lined with cat hair. At first I listened politely, still restraining my son from the shelves, but then the woman began to exceed her minute and my daughter's whine progressed to a howl. Did that stop my PETA pal? No she just pressed on. If I had ever thought about looking into her charges I wasn't going to do so after that run in. In fact, her story lost credibility because she didn't come across as someone who had simple good sense.

The lesson here is that you simply have to recognize when to put the brakes on what appears to be a lucky break. In order to respect other people's boundaries you should do the following:

- **Listen:** Is someone trying to tell you it's not the right time? Don't force-feed them information. They'll just spit it out.
- **Read the situation:** Is the person you want to reach with her family? Is she in the midst of a fun activity? Is the person in a potentially embarrassing circumstance (say, the shower!)? Then this is not business as usual.
- **Read body language:** Is the person you want to approach clearly distracted (perhaps trying to control his children) while trying to be nice? It's a good time to say, "Hey, you're obviously busy now. When can I call?"

### You Never Know Whom You're Talking To . . .

A *Wall Street Journal* article entitled *Do-It-Yourself Consulting: CEOs Gather to Swap Tips* (July 26, 2007) told the story of a CEO who needed to make some staff cuts. He invited a friend, a top executive from another firm, to his company Christmas party. At the end of the party, his peer made suggestions about whom he should fire. Obviously, some employees were slacking off in the "first impression" department.

The moral of the story: If you are at *any* work-related function, have your boilerplate ready for when you meet someone you don't know. Maintain a conversational style, and be sensitive to social boundaries.

## First Minute, First Impression

No doubt you've heard about the importance of making a good first impression. This is more than folklore or mannerly advice from the etiquette-happy; this is hard scientific fact. Psychological studies show that we make rapid assessments of one anther on first encounters, and begin predicting the future of a relationship with someone as soon as we begin communicating with him. While subsequent contacts might alter our opinion, the first impression is extremely powerful in determining if we even want further contact.

In fact, a negative first impression carries more weight than a positive one. If one party thinks the relationship has low potential to bring any kind of satisfaction, there is often little the other party can do to secure a chance to change the other person's mind.

You can easily make a very *good* impression in the course of a minute. You must manage each minute well but the first one best of all. With luck—no, make that with *effort* and *attention*—this will lead to opportunities for you to get your message across in an even more comprehensive and detailed way.

## Top Tips

1. Remember the one-minute message formula: Say who you are, what you do, and why you do it better.
2. Respect boundaries—be sensitive to the setting and make sure your potential listener wants to hear what you want to share at that particular time.
3. When you have a minute, the anecdote/story is the best way to back up your point—and keep that conversational tone.

# Meeting Modules

## THE MEETING MEAT WITHOUT THE FAT

It's no secret that we are all meeting more and enjoying it less. And whether we attend PTA or charity meetings or high-pressure C-level meetings filled with movers and shakers, our primary complaint is probably the same: Where is the meat? Oftentimes, it seems that no one knows how to be concise. Because of this, generally we feel bloated and unsatisfied when the meetings end.

If you want to come off well at a meeting and be the one participant everyone admires, listens to and, indeed, the one marked for bigger and better things, you need a format that will allow you to deliver your news effectively and efficiently.

You need a five-minute meeting module. That's what this chapter is all about.

### The Five-Minute Formula: Meeting Meat without the Fat

The majority of meetings involve updates. A number of people are expected to say what they have been doing and what they plan to do. Sometimes they add a pitch for an idea or a request for resources. If you don't have a structure for presenting this information you are all too likely to get bogged down in details, to go off on tangents, and to invite repeated interruption. The solution: Come prepared with five minutes of relevant, comprehensive, and seamless content.

In the last chapter I outlined the one-minute elevator module. Sandwiched between a brief opening and a closing call to action are three message points, but only one proof, that is, a very quick example or anecdote to sell your points. Similarly, the five-minute meeting module is also a headline and call to action sandwich, but stuffed with meatier filling.

Now you can provide a proof for each of your points in the form of a fact, a story, or possibly an analogy:

| | |
|---|---|
| Headline | What's your topic? |
| Three Message Points | What's new? |
|    Message Point 1 | Include 1 proof |
|    Message Point 2 | Include 1 proof |
|    Message Point 3 | Include 1 proof |
| Call to Action | What do you need from the others at the meeting? |

This might seem like a lot of material to deliver in five minutes. But as with your one-minute message, if you get out your timer and try it, you will see it works very well. (For writing purposes, remember that one typewritten double-spaced page is one minute.)

### Stand and Deliver

A partner at one of the best-known private equity firms, where no one suffers fools for a New York minute (let alone for five minutes), once told me he was desperate to get his team to cut to the chase. Updating deals at meetings was an ordeal. He began having them use my five-minute formula. If they started wandering off the top he would demand, "What is your headline?" and then he took it one step farther. He had everyone stand up to deliver their updates.

Standing tends to make people more concise. And, because studies show that people gain credibility, persuasive power, and, yes, stature when they stand, you should choose to stand up to present at meetings whenever you can.

## Meeting Jousts: Disarming Your Challengers

In terms of what content you choose to include there is an important differentiator between the one-minute elevator module and the five-minute meeting module. When you are delivering a one-minute elevator module it's unlikely that you'll be challenged. When you are in a meeting, it is likely that you *will* be challenged. That means that you have to focus first on the highlights of what you have done (this is no time for modesty) and tightly support your rationale with facts and anecdotes. Then you must anticipate all the questions about what you haven't done.

That's right. There will always be someone in your meeting who will be ready to put you on the defensive. Sure, you will probably get some pushback from your boss. It is part of his job. But challenges are almost as likely to come from coworkers with differing agendas: someone who wants to look good by making you look bad, a nitpicker who thrives by focusing on minutia, or a risk-averse naysayer who doesn't want to go forward with any plan at all. So ask yourself the hard questions. Why is this project over budget? Why is this deal delayed? Why didn't I touch base with human resources? Is this really a good opportunity? It is always easier to make the answers part of *your* story than to wait until you are up against the ropes.

For example, I was working with a newly promoted communications executive, John, whose job involved working with advertising and promotions people at a Los Angeles-based clothing company. Without John's input, the advertising and promotions staff had come up with ideas and events designed to promote a new maternity fashion line. They spent a great deal of money and then expected John to drum up press coverage on short notice. One problem was that their guest list included no "A" list celebrities, which made it extremely difficult to interest feature reporters in L.A. Another problem was that the event was scheduled for a Saturday, a day when news staffs are limited.

In John's first meeting with the ad team, they described their upcoming event in glowing detail. Then all eyes turned to John. The fact was he'd contacted all the appropriate members of the press without getting any coverage commitments. He said as much, and left it at that, leaving a rather bad impression. With another update meeting on the near horizon and with nothing likely to change, John contacted me for help. I helped him to develop a headline that said in an honest way that he foresaw problems with the event. We then developed a three-point rubric for judging the news value of anything:

1. Was it new?
2. Was the timing right?
3. Were there big names involved?

Then I had him insert an anecdote about why some particular members of the press had declined to cover the maternity fashion event (none of the really "hot" celebrities was pregnant right now!). This meeting went much better for John, as did future ones. His three-point rubric allowed him to discuss all upcoming events in a systematic, less personalized way. Ultimately he got so good at educating the promotion and ad teams that he was brought in early to help design events.

## Back Pocket Modules

Of course, no matter how well you prepare, there is always a chance that you will be interrupted by someone who wants more in the form of proof. When I was in the news business, I had a boss who brought the art of brevity to a new high. As soon as you would start to speak, he would start a timer. Then he would interrupt you to boot.

The meetings I prepared hardest for were the ones where we had to justify what stories we would put on the air during ratings sweeps. I would present a rationale for why I should be able to do, for example, a series on school board corruption rather than the standard "killer salad bar" segment (you know the kind: "What's the bacteria count on that three-day-old hard boiled egg?"). I'd start my school board pitch and my boss would interject, "Who cares?" and "How do you know?" Colleagues interested in the killer salad bars would look sour, or bored, and bring up the cost of tracking corrupt school board members. Why bother when those deadly salad bars were on every other corner? To combat their inquiries, I'd be ready with facts and anecdotes.

**Who cares?** Our audience does. It wastes their tax dollars. It affects their lives. Here's how it affected one family (anecdote).

**How do you know?** We have special access to these people and places (fact).

I learned from this type of firing line experience that you should always go to a meeting with extra stories and facts in your back pocket. The stories help people see relevance and connect to a concept. The facts (these can be in many forms, including studies, surveys, or polls) show that you are credible and that you have done your homework.

## Know Who's Across the Table

When presenting at meetings, as in all other presentation situations, it is imperative that you know who is likely to show up. A lot of people make the mistake of showing up with the same five minutes of material regardless of who will be across the table. That violates the first rule of the communications tripod: Know your audience.

Recycling the same old material can be distinctly counterproductive. A client of mine owned a small chain of ultra expensive clothing boutiques. When a large department store bought her business, her employees worried that work wouldn't be as rewarding. They also feared that they would lose customers because they didn't think the department store managers understood them. A top executive visited the boutiques' design room in hopes of assuring the team that they take care of good customers, too. He offered an anecdote about a unique basement sale the department store offered its big spenders.

This story worked with other audiences, but it fell flat with his new employees. Indeed, it reinforced their fears that he was clueless about what appealed to their wealthy customers. The executive probably would have been better off with an anecdote praising a specific service the boutique provided; maybe the hoops they'd jumped through to make sure Ms. Done-well had her custom gown in time for the gala.

As far as Jane and her associates were concerned, their new boss would have been better off without any anecdote at all. This one did more harm than good, as it reinforced their fears. It also gave the impression that the speaker didn't care about them enough to find a new story.

## Boilerplates Can Land You in Hot Water

Trotting out a worn anecdote over and over can do even more harm than making your audience feel misunderstood. Another danger is that you might begin to bore yourself, resulting in a flat delivery. Very few of us are like Broadway actors, able to deliver the same lines day after day, night after night, and sound sincere. We are doing well if we can do it once!

# Meeting with Style

Meetings are filled with many faces, some friendly, interested, and approving—some not. You need to be effective in delivering your five-minute meeting module despite any bored or sour faces. My experience suggests that women have an especially tough time with the negative vibes, even when there are only a few people emitting them. When I was young, if there was one sour face in the audience, I would focus on that one person and try to bring him around. In time, I learned to do what my male reporter friends seemed to do more naturally than I, that is, focus on the majority of friendly faces and on the top decision makers.

You might also be faced with people who talk or whisper when you present at meetings. If so, consider the power of body language. If you are standing, as I think you should be, walk around the table and stand behind the offenders or ask one of them a question. I guarantee that the offenders will not only stop offending but also that others will think twice about chatting during your presentation.

Finally, make sure your phrasing and your tone are right for your audience. Think of your meeting style as light, medium, or heavy:

## Me First

If you can speak first at a meeting, do so. This puts you in position to be proactive rather than reactive. If you are scheduled to speak late in the meeting you might find your time usurped by a long-winded colleague. However, if that happens, you can often get a reprieve and save your slot by promising, "I'll just be five minutes." And so you will!

- Light = Relaxed and informal, perhaps amusing.
- Medium = Polite and straightforward (safest, especially with people you don't know well).
- Heavy = Faster paced, just the facts, short and crisp.

Think of these as three roads to meeting success, each with a different speed limit.

No matter what the emotional temperature of the room, it is important that you keep your presentation fresh and keep your audience in mind. Even if you have said similar things before, remember that it may be the first time that members of your audience are hearing you or your presentation's content. So hit the "refresh" button.

## Top Tips

1. Time yourself and you will see that five minutes is plenty of time to deliver a headline, three message points with one proof apiece, and a call to action.
2. Have extra facts and anecdotes or stories handy to handle challenges.
3. Let your style suit the meeting tone: ascertain if the gathering is informal, more businesslike, or a hard-hitting, speedy power meeting.

# CHAPTER 10

# Main Attraction Modules

Just as everyone in business will at some point have use for one-minute and five-minute messages, it is virtually assured that at some time in your career you will be asked to give a longer presentation. This chapter will explain, step by step, how to organize and deliver a longer talk that will not *feel* long to your listeners.

By the way, in most cases, "longer" means about 20 minutes. For most topics, this amount of time is more than sufficient to give an engaging, comprehensive talk. In fact, if I ruled the world I would probably have a law that said that no one should present for longer than 20 minutes. However, I don't rule the world (just ask my teenage children) and so it might well be the case that at some point you will be requested to give a presentation that will last 30 minutes, 45 minutes, or even an hour.

Don't panic. The important tripod rules of making presentations and delivering information are still the same: Know what your audience cares about, give them content that is fresh, and sell it with style. In a day when technology is king, and PowerPoint reigns, ideas still trump all. If something interests and surprises *you*, and gets *you* enthusiastic, your message will be heard. Think hard about what you have to say that is new or different, and be courageous enough to say it. (As Margaret Thatcher said, "Win the argument and you win the election.")

Thus, the true challenge with a long—or longer—presentation is knowing what to put in and, just as critical, what to leave out.

## Kitchen Sinks Not Required—Just the Garbage Disposal

The temptation, especially with presentations exceeding 20 minutes in length, is to throw in everything including the kitchen sink. Why offer up three message points when you have time for six, ten, or twenty! Don't give in to this temptation. Remember in a world short of attention spans, more is usually less.

The basic rule of thumb for a 20-minute presentation is to allow a total of five minutes for your open (consisting of a greeting, headline, and context) and your close (consisting of a summary and call to action). Because signposts only take a few seconds, the remaining 15 minutes are devoted to your three message points and their proofs. In other words, you get approximately five minutes to make each point with facts, analogies, and anecdotes.

| | |
|---|---|
| Open and Close combined | 5 minutes |
| Message Point 1 | 5 minutes |
| Message Point 2 | 5 minutes |
| Message Point 3 | 5 minutes |

If you've got 45 minutes or an hour you should still allot approximately five minutes total to open and close, and still center your talk on three—and only three—message points. People simply will not remember more, even if you talk to them all day.

Naturally, I hear from clients all the time that they *can't* narrow their message points down to three when they have twenty. Oh yes, they can—and they do—by following a simple technique: using a flip chart.

To start, get out a flip chart and start listing those 20 messages. Then, draw lines between the ones that have a natural connection. Soon, you will find you can almost always group them into three categories. For instance, if you list the following messages:

1. We have a new dynamic manager of IT who has made a name for herself in the tech world.
2. We just developed a new system that is improving workers' productivity.
3. We just developed a flexible work initiative.

You should notice that all three fall under "We are attracting and keeping great talent."

If you have a stray point that simply does not fit, ask yourself if it really belongs in this particular presentation.

## Creating Your Modules in Order

Sometimes the hardest part of preparing a long presentation is knowing where to begin. The order in which you write your modules can vary to some degree, but the headline should always come first. To recap, the headline strategies offered in Chapter 5 were:

- Focus in on the one thing you most want your audience to grasp.
- Include an element of surprise.
- Keep your headline simple and direct.

Once a headline is in place, tackle your three message points next. If you start with these it is far less likely that you will ramble as you go along. The three message points give depth and detail to the headline. Now you have a framework around which to build the rest of your talk, regardless of its length.

But just how do you come up with the rest of your modules?

## Coming Up with a Context Module

Next, let's look at creating a context for your message. Context is a brief but important module that provides some history or background that puts a message in perspective. In order to uncover the context of something, you may ask yourself, "Where are we and how did we get here? Who are you and what is your experience? Context is especially useful when you are saying what you can do that is new. That's because it tells what the situation is now. In other words, you always have to define the disease before anyone will buy the cure.

Suppose your message is: "We cannot think only about sales; we must also focus on profits." For people to grasp this concept, your context module could show the recent trend in sales, alongside a record of shrinking margins. People will grasp the problem when they hear the impact on the company's cash flow. ("We are all happy with our widget sales right? But do you know how much we actually clear after costs?")

If, as another example, you run a charity where contributions have been declining, you have to show they've been declining for a significant period (it's more than a seasonal blip) and by how much before you can propose a solution. If you are claiming that a school needs a curriculum change, you will need to note the problems that have occurred while the old curriculum has been in place such as lower standardized test scores.

A word of caution: You don't need to overdo context. Along with your headline it should not comprise more than two to three minutes of your total time, no matter how long your talk. History is important, and we do need to learn from it, but the bulk of your presentation should be about what to do today that will impact tomorrow.

## Creating a Catchy Signpost

In the course of preparing your longer presentation, be on the lookout for brief, catchy phrases that could end up as signposts. A signpost is like a mantra: a refrain or phrase that is simple, memorable, and even a tad hypnotic. Its repetition helps you steadily build your argument. With each repetition you are saying, *"See what I mean!?"*

The signpost should appeal to people's sense of logic. It should make your audience raise their eyebrows and nod, "Yup!" After Hillary Clinton lost the primary in Iowa she came out swinging at Barack Obama with a signpost. In her speech she delivered a list of examples where she claimed Obama said one thing and did another, and after each item, she repeated "that's not change." The signpost helped her build her case.

Effective signposts often use little literary devices. Sometimes they rhyme (*If the glove doesn't fit, you must acquit*). Sometimes they are alliterative, repeating the same starting sound (a school board candidate disgruntled with "new math" and lack of grammar education campaigned with the signpost: *Bring back the basics*). But such devices are not strictly necessary as long as your phrasing is simple and punchy.

Bear in mind that your signpost can't be too specific. It needs to be versatile and broad enough to apply to all three of your message points. Think of a tagline like that used by an advertising agency. A line like, "It's what makes a Subaru, a Subaru" would work in a speech to address all aspects of the driving experience: aesthetics (the look of the car), mechanics (the performance of the car), and people (the teams that design and build the car). Think of the BP ad line, "There's energy security in energy diversity." In a speech, an executive for an oil company could use that line to discuss geographic diversity (drilling globally to ensure a secure supply), sources of energy (oil, gas, wind, solar, nuclear) and research (exploring new fuels).

## If You Own It, You Can Use It

If you are coming up short on ideas or time, consider appropriating your ad line as a signpost. You paid for it already! The important thing is that the line supports your message.

## Proof Positive: Finding Facts, Analogies, and Anecdotes

The upside of a long presentation is that you should have adequate time to offer proofs for each of your three message points. Remember, ideally you should have a fact, an analogy, and an anecdote for each (3 × 3 = memory).

### About Facts

Facts are probably the easiest type of proof to come up with. Your own organization should have an inventory of relevant metrics and customer testimonials. And remember, in addition to numbers, facts can also be accolades that you have won, a quote from you in a well-regarded journal or newspaper, or a quote *about* you from a credible source.

Facts are most memorable when they are new and surprising. But facts won't work at all unless they are, well, factual. Facts about virtually any industry or area of interest are now just a Google search away. But be sure to check facts gathered from cyberspace. Anyone can create a web site and anyone can contribute to

Wikipedia. Always look for corroboration from a second source if your fact is at all in doubt. And because any audience can have a self-appointed fact checker, mark facts with an asterisk and have a reference handy in case you're asked, "Where did you get that?"

### About Analogies

Analogies require you to think outside your world and ask: *What is this like?* Analogies work quite well if you are trying to get people to try something new and you can convince them it is like something else they have already accepted. For example, in the film *Sicko*, director Michael Moore reassured his audience that universal government-sponsored health care was not such an odd thing—after all, he said, we have universal government-sponsored education. (I'll let you decide which argument this analogy supported.)

I was working with the CEO of a company that manufactures new energy-efficient lightbulbs. Although they can save money and energy, they have to be disposed of carefully. If they break or when they run out of juice, the consumer is supposed to box them up and ship them somewhere. Okay, said the CEO, that is *like* recycling. It wasn't so long ago that we would have balked at separating out our gooey glass and smelly plastic bottles and taking them to a recycling center or at least to the end of the driveway. Now we do it weekly.

Because analogies can make a point quickly, advertisers rely on them heavily. Accenture, a business technology consulting firm came up with an ad with a field of sunflowers yet to bloom except for one. The ad reads, "Outsourcing from Accenture can help you outperform expectations." Translation: Your business will be blooming while others are snoozing. So peruse print ads or channel surf for TV ads if you are in need of inspiration.

### Using Reverse Analogies

The head of a major pharmaceutical firm was having a tough time convincing people that importing medicines from other countries over the Internet posed any kind of threat. So he used a reverse analogy. Instead of saying what something was like, he said what it was *unlike*. "Medicines aren't like fruit. You can't pick it up, look at it, and tell if it is good. You have to trust the system it came through."

### About Anecdotes

To come up with an anecdote, ask yourself: How does what you do affect one person, one client, one customer, one victim, one beneficiary? Ask, "Give me an example." Then ask yourself the same thing several more times until you come up with the kind of granularity you need for a good story. Details enable the listener to picture what you are saying and it really doesn't take more time to do it right. I call this the Storytelling Formula (see Figure 10.1).

As you can see in Figure 10.1, the CEO of Staples was on CNBC talking about how they had just spent a lot of money putting computers in every store that allowed salespeople and customers to quickly access warehouse supplies. Now many would stop with the explanation right there, but does that conjure up an image in your mind? I'll bet not. Instead, the CEO explained the wisdom of improving technology through the experience of one customer. He said:

- We had a school teacher at our store in Indianapolis who needed 200 red binders.
- We have more supplies than just about anyone else but we didn't have 200 red binders in that store.
- We were able to hook her up to the Internet and have the binders delivered to her school the next day.

You can use the same formula to deliver your anecdote.

News stories almost always rely on anecdotes. Little stories sell big points. They are the best way to explain complex issues. Pick up

- Set the stage

- Pinpoint the problem

- Sell your solution

- Do it in 30 seconds

**Figure 10.1    Storytelling Formula**

any newspaper and you will see how virtually every complex issue is explained with the story of one—one person, one family, one business, one customer. One can tell the tale of thousands, even millions.

When I reported a story on a new budget revealing millions spent on maintaining New York City public housing buildings, I broke the figure down to a number per apartment in a typical building. (Otherwise budget numbers are so big they mean nothing.) My computation came out to roughly $10,000 per apartment. Then I found one family—that of a hardworking mom who cleaned other houses for a living—who showed me her apartment's missing tiles and holes in her walls. That drove home the point, *Where is all the money going?*

### Using Humor

Anecdotes often provide an opportunity to incorporate humor into your talk. I tell my clients to avoid jokes (not all are funny to everyone, and even professional comedians flop routinely. Why take the risk?) But I'm all for using humor when it can lighten a mood, reinforce a point, and help people relate to you and your news.

A detailed granular anecdote is concise and emotional—but not *too* emotional and not *too* granular. When I worked with the March of Dimes, I encouraged its spokespeople to be concise. To parents, every moment and graphic detail of their child's medical saga is important, and understandably so. Still, the audience has an attention limit. Every story needs a past ("My daughter had a premature birth. She could be held in my husband's palm."), a present ("Today she is six, a *tae kwon do* master, and the apple of my eye.") and a connection to your message ("Help the March of Dimes establish more neonatal intensive care units like the one that helped save our baby.").

## Rehearsing for Long Presentations

It's crucial to rehearse for your long presentation. Doing so will help you clarify your thoughts, fine-tune your talk, and feel more relaxed. But reading silently through your script won't do the trick. Instead, you must do the following:

- Mark words to stress.
- Note where to smile.
- Note where to move.
- Mark where to pause.

Then do it as if for real. Stand up and act as if *this is it.*

If you can line up a colleague to watch you or—better yet—to videotape you, so much the better. I know that might seem painful, but no pain, no gain. Besides, many people who see themselves on tape find it a source of confidence building. They don't look nearly as bad as they thought they did and they identify what they can do better!

## Cutting It Short?

Finally, as you go over your presentation, change lines that don't read well. (If you can't repeat you must delete!) Mark what you can cut or condense. No matter how much time has been formally allotted to you, there are circumstances when you will want to streamline a long speech. Such circumstances can include:

- When others before you have gone on too long.
- When the time of day is late and people are getting groggy.
- When people have sat through a long dinner.
- When people are hungry and dying to *get* to dinner.
- When there are lots of awards to be given out.
- When people are chomping at the bit to get to the next speaker.

Use your eyes, ears, and instincts to ascertain when your audience is too restless, tired, or impatient to absorb a message presented in an extended format. If that is the case, you will do your listeners—and yourself—a favor by modifying your modules. Keep the parts that are most surprising and most emotional (this usually means hanging on to your anecdotal proofs and your call to action) and shorten or cut your factual proofs, historical context, and summary. Remember the beauty of a modular message is its flexibility. If you can't use all your time, make the most of time you can use.

## Top Tips

1. For a 20-minute talk, allow roughly 5 minutes for each message point and 5 minutes—combined—for your opening and closing.
2. Look to the advertising world for inspiration for analogies. For anecdotes, get granular. Ask yourself: How does what you do affect one person, one customer, one employee?
3. It's crucial to rehearse for long presentations. Don't just mouth it to yourself; stand up and do it as if this were the real deal.

# The Power to Cure PowerPoint and Master Other Visual Aids

Homer said, "The mind is more slowly stirred by the ear than by the eye." We say, "A picture is worth a thousand words." Although these two phrases are from different centuries, their overall meaning is generally the same: that is, visuals are powerful. We know this instinctively, and science backs up our instincts with studies that show:

- Seventy-five percent of what we learn comes to us visually.
- Visuals double the length of time we remember things.
- Words with pictures are six times more effective than words alone.

Nevertheless, as this chapter will show, the power of visuals—like virtually all other potent powers—can be used for good or for ill. Visuals can enhance your message and make it memorable, or they can usurp it, distract from it, or even derail it. Perhaps nowhere is this more evident than in a presentation that incorporates the world's most infamous, most ubiquitous slideware: PowerPoint.

## PowerPoint: Use It; Don't Be Used by It

In corporate America, in government agencies, even in our schools, several hundred million copies of Microsoft PowerPoint are churning out trillions of slides each year. Is this a good thing? It depends whom you ask.

In a famous *Wired* magazine editorial entitled, "PowerPoint Is Evil," Edward Tufte, a Yale political science and computer science professor, said the application's emphasis on format over content commercializes and trivializes subjects for adults and has children developing bullets instead of strong sentences. Internet pioneer Vint Cerf likes to quip, "Power corrupts. PowerPoint corrupts absolutely." A fellow coach calls PowerPoint the most misused technological invention since the handgun. And, as audience members, we have all experienced death by PowerPoint, the comatose state that results from being subjected to one stultifying slide after another.

The killing fields are everywhere, from think tanks to grade school classrooms to corporate boardrooms turned "bored-rooms." And the reason is simply that PowerPoint is convenient and easy. You don't have to prepare or practice as much. You don't have to think as much. And *that* is often the problem.

It is my contention that PowerPoint isn't bad *per se*. I use it in my training sessions. What is bad about PowerPoint is the way we too often use it and have allowed ourselves to be used *by* the technology. However, I do believe we are turning the corner. I see instances where some of the best presenters are beginning to use this infamous application in ways that actually increase understanding and memory and manage to entertain all at the same time. And that is the point!

### Using the Tool

Al Gore connected to a diverse audience in *An Inconvenient Truth* with revealing and varied slides that used vivid images and few words. He made sure the technology did not overwhelm him. He and his key message (the climate crisis can be solved) remained the focal points. Gore was not upstaged by his own technology.

PowerPoint should be used to make *your* points. But too many presenters put the cart before the horse. They ask, "What slides do I have?" before asking "What do I want to say and how can I say it best?" They give the tool the power. They forgo what could be art in order to paint by numbers.

## Slide Content: The Good, the Bad, and the Ugly

I spent a day in Detroit working with the CEO of an automobile engineering firm, helping him prepare for a big speech on how his company had dramatically improved the quality of its products and won billions in new business. The first thing he did was look at a slide set his quality team had prepared. The large slide deck was packed with facts and figures that supported how many units they'd sold a few years ago compared with today and that enumerated new customers. The CEO criticized the slides for missing his point and his team began talking about how to improve them or talk around them. I interrupted and insisted on knowing what exactly he wanted to say. I advised him to open without a slide by saying where the company was today—what and how they were doing—versus where they were five years ago. Improvement captures attention, and you don't need a slide to get it. Next, I advised him to detail three things—just three—that improved the picture. Finally, I told him to close without slides, saying where the company is going and how it will get there. Only when he had this structure in place should he consider how, and where, slides could support his message.

This executive's initial approach illustrates some of the fundamental mistakes presenters make with regard to PowerPoint:

1. **He looked to the slides to lead content.** This CEO was a dynamic leader, yet he was prepared to follow a trail of slideware like a bird picking up stray breadcrumbs. Your ideas and your news should always lead. PowerPoint should support and embellish.
2. **He planned to start with a slide even before he said, "Hello."** Don't ever launch PowerPoint before letting the audience connect with you. The audience is there to see and hear the speaker. Even if you have your agenda on a slide, have a

separate open. I have seen presenters greet the audience and read their own names from a slide. How do you think that makes the audience feel? They may well wonder if you really are pleased to be there or if you know your own title. In the same vein, do your close—especially your call to action—sans slides. I call this bookending your presentation with eye contact.

3. **He planned to use slides that were busy and distracting.** Too many numbers or too many images add up to nothing but confusion. Data-laden slides detract from the speaker. The audience can easily get lost in them and will stop listening to you. If you can't let go of a busy slide, consider item-by-item reveals, and fade items you don't want the audience to focus on anymore. Consider pointing to one item and say, "I want you just to focus on this point for one minute and let me give you a little insight." Then you might take a few steps away and begin to explain. Finally, you can simply hit "B" on your keyboard to black out the slide. It is another way to jolt the audience and reel your listeners back in by requiring they look to you for information. If there are details you want on the slides for the audience to pore over later, think about having two decks: one streamlined for your presentation and one more detailed to be used as a handout after you speak.

4. **He didn't plan to vary his types of slides.** Slide after slide of facts and figures is a surefire recipe for creating boredom and inattentiveness. Use images, cartoons, and ads. Mix it up. (I recently received a PowerPoint deck from a client, a fancy business consulting firm. It was 93 slides and not one image! All data. It's no wonder the firm's marketing people wanted help to boil it down for a customer pitch they'd caught!)

In Figure 11.1, I provide a comparison between a message conveyed using a graph and a picture. A pharmaceutical company wanted to show that the percentage of the health care dollar spent on prescription drugs is smaller than many think. When they came to me, they showed me the graph you see in Figure 11.1a, which they had been using. Instead, I told them to convey this same message with a picture, supported by data in Figure 11.1b. Same message but one is more memorable.

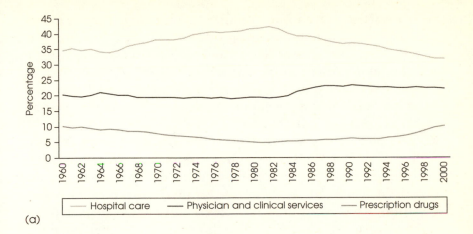

(a)

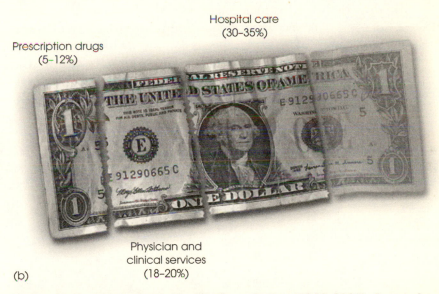

Hospital care
(30–35%)

Prescription drugs
(5–12%)

Physician and
clinical services
(18–20%)

(b)

**Figure 11.1    The Nation's Health Care Dollar (1960–2001): Percentage Spent by Category (a) Graph Message vs. (b). Picture It, Remember It**

5. **He started with too many slides.** I urge clients to figure an average of one minute per slide (some slides will require a bit more time, some less). That's about 15 slides for your average 20-minute presentation leaving time for your open and close. Aim for a maximum of three to five points per slide and three to five words per point. Avoid complete sentences. The audience should literally look to you for elaboration.

6. **Everyone can read, don't do it for them.** Another mistake I warned this CEO against was reading his slides verbatim. Don't read everything you say. A recent *Wall Street Journal* article likened this common problem to "corporate karaoke." If this is a familiar tune, you might as well have e-mailed the deck to everyone rather than hosting yet another meeting. People want to hear your interpretation, not a recitation of the information on the slide. Occasionally you should try previewing, that is, introducing a slide *before* showing it, by asking a question like, "So what do you think that did to our sales, up how much?" This technique is commonly used in the movies where you hear the train before your see it. It adds drama. (Please note, this requires having a hard copy of your presentation in front of you, which is also a good idea for when technical glitches occur, as they are wont to do.)

---

### Staying on Track

If you are used to having data on every slide it is all right to wean yourself slowly. If you spend too much time talking over a wordless image you could get lost. Plan to make one point while showing the image and then list additional points in text on the following slide.

---

I have also found that if you are too wed to the words on your slides you will have a tendency to bury your lines as you look down to change slides. Advancing your slides offers you an easy opportunity to pause and look up, to make eye contact with your audience, to gauge the mood in the room, and to pace yourself. As Mozart said, "The silence between the notes is as important as the notes themselves."

## Point and Release

Watch out for those laser pointers. Too often it turns into a "follow the bouncing ball" exercise —irritating and distracting. Try balancing your hand with the pointer on top of your free hand to hold it steady. Point briefly to what you want to highlight; then release and elaborate. Say, "This fact is the most important in my view and let me tell you why . . ." You can then click the "B" on your keyboard to blacken the screen temporarily, or simply walk away from the slide, perhaps to the other side of the room so that the audience's eyes follow you. Now you are directing the pace at which the audience consumes information. You remain in charge of the technology.

## Talk Back to Me: Visuals as a Road to Interactivity

No PowerPoint presentation, no matter how skillfully done, will have the desired effect if it does not engage the audience. One slide following another and another gets to be a snore even if each slide taken individually is interesting. Engagement is imperative. That's why one of the main trends in presentations today is making room for more interactivity.

Your PowerPoint-based presentation—or indeed any presentation using visuals—can offer excellent opportunities to engage your audience in an interactive way. Look through visuals for opportunities to:

- Turn facts into a quiz.
- Ask a rhetorical question ("Have you ever seen numbers like this before?").
- Ask a responsive question.
- Take a poll by asking for a show of hands.
- Ask for reactions.
- Ask for agreement.

Achieving interactivity involves more than casually saying, "Hey, feel free to jump in and ask a question." You'll need to go through your text ahead of time and mark places to reach out to the audience. Then, during your talk, it's a good idea to keep track of who has and hasn't spoken so that you can make a point of drawing out people who are silent, shy, or simply would-be snoozers.

But the most important thing to remember about interactivity is that it all begins with an attitude—*your* attitude. If you are used to being a didactic speaker you will have to change the way you have always done things. Spouting information is a one-way street. Interactivity is a two-way street—trickier to negotiate, but more accessible.

To be successfully interactive you have to relinquish some degree of control. You have to accept the fact that you may not have all the answers or that an audience member might contribute something you didn't think of first. And you have to be courageous enough to allow for spontaneity. But the benefits of increased understanding and engagement outweigh the risks of feeling less than king of the mountain. When you involve your audience, people stay awake and alert; more than that, they feel valued. In the end, even with a few detours, you get your message across.

## Should You Go with Video?

Now, let's get back to technology itself. If you think that PowerPoint slides are your only option for presentations, think again. Video is being used more and more. Video is a powerful tool that makes for a memorable message, but it should be used with care. Like a strong cologne, a little dab'll do ya. With video, you should be thinking in seconds. Remember this important new rule: 30 to 90 seconds per clip is enough. *15 seconds is ideal.*

In addition, use video to make a *main* point, and one that is *positive.* One pharmaceutical client of mine is very marketing savvy, but its top executives sometimes misuse video. One, for example, developed a dramatic three-minute video that showed despoiled environments around the globe and talked about how this company did *its* share of polluting. While dramatic, the piece was too long and did not underscore his more important point: this company had done so much to clean up its act it had won a prestigious award. At one point in his talk he mentioned how company manufacturing plants had changed the way they operated in order to be more "green." *That* is what he should have supported with video because that was what he wanted remembered.

A lot of people are intimidated by the technology of video and believe any video piece has to be professionally edited. But that's not necessarily the case. A commercial real estate client of mine, a top-selling saleswoman, says what she offers is market intelligence. To make her point, she carries a small video camera with her and grabs a little footage of, say, traffic patterns in front of a building to show this is *not* the best building in which to buy. Her clips are short, but prove her point better than any narrative.

Taking and showing video is usually simple enough. But be sure to do a run-through that includes a "let's go to the videotape" segue so you are sure what button to push when. If you took your video with a handheld camera make sure the image is not blurry, and not too "jumpy" or you'll have to hand out Dramamine before your talk. This is a business presentation after all, not the *Blair Witch Project*.

## React with Your Audience

If you're showing a video clip, look at it *with* your audience, and—even if you have seen it a million times—react as if you just saw it as they did. Don't bury your head in your script to see what is next. I once worked with an executive team to develop moving videos of patients who'd benefited from their drug research. The video's emotional impact was diluted when the presenter who introduced the clip didn't even glance at it playing over his shoulder.

## The Art of the Flip Chart

Visuals don't have to be high tech to make a lasting impression. Research shows that people remember items like bar graphs or bell curves drawn on a flip chart longer than they remember computer-generated graphics. The act of watching the presenter create the data in real time is engaging and enhances credibility as a leader if not as an artist. The flip chart is also effective for underscoring a message. We've talked about the value of asking questions. Why not tally the yes's and no's on a flip chart or capture guesses on how much sales increased after a new product improvement; then circle the winner. People love games and you'll win the challenge of getting people to remember your message. The big caveat here is to make sure your audience can see the chart. If there are more than 30 people in the room, you might need to reconsider.

When using flip charts, it's a good idea to sketch information like numbers in light pencil before presenting (thereby creating your own private crib sheet). Be sure not to talk and write at the same time or you won't project well and you'll lose all-important eye contact.

Always turn to talk to your audience. If you are right-handed, the flip chart should be on your left. Point to information with your left hand. If you feel uncomfortable getting up from a conversation to use a flip-chart, you can use a piece of paper to reinforce a main point.

## The Power of Props

Remember your favorite science classes in school? The most memorable days were the ones where the teacher made hard-boiled eggs turn purple or created one of those vinegar-and-baking soda volcanoes. Props! That was the ticket. Props also used to be popular in business presentations, but with the rise of PowerPoint and digital pictures they started to vanish. Now they are beginning to make a comeback.

At first you might feel a little silly using props. Isn't that for magicians who pull rabbits out of top hats? But even though this practice might not be in your comfort zone, it works. Props are a way to move the needle. Who can forget Colin Powell holding a model vial of anthrax while giving a presentation to the United Nations Security Council, or Tim Russert on election night with his little handheld eraser board and marker.

The use of props for business presentations is also on the rise. Recently, I was working with a consumer goods company and an executive brought in a little model to show how they were purifying water and making a difference. It was dramatic and effective. (In fact, it seemed a little like one of those spellbinding science classes!)

In another instance, I was working with a printing company that sells customized checks. The checks are used a lot less today than they were 20 or 30 years ago, because they are being eclipsed by newer products like debit cards. Still, they are selling a lot and one executive decided to energize the team of people who work on checks by unveiling a huge pile of them to illustrate how many they sell globally everyday. The point: Yes, we are selling fewer, but we are still selling a heck of a lot! This, too, worked. It was surprising. It made people smile and respect the leader who did something a little differently to make a point that was important to them.

Props don't need to be elaborate to be effective. I worked with a top executive at a credit card company who wanted to make the point that credit cards are being used to purchase everyday items. He brought his morning cup of coffee and bagel to a meeting and showed the credit card he'd used to buy them at a store across the street. I also work with a commercial real estate team that routinely prints out its PowerPoint presentations on big strips of paper that they roll out for the customer during the presentation. This mixed-media approach turns what might have been staid slideware into an interactive activity.

The point is to think creatively about what can best be used to send your message. The best presenters are beginning to turn a corner and get creative with all kinds of visual aids. Visuals, used well, can be yet another way to *jolt so they don't bolt.*

## No Substitute for Hands On

Introducing a new product? Bring it. People want to touch it. Pass it—or at least a model of it—around the room. Show the breakthrough hearing aid, the cool MP3 player, and the stylized faucet. Let people sit in the new, more comfortable airline seat. You can use all the high-tech presentation tricks you want, but sometimes nothing beats high-touch to get people excited. (When you go to an Apple store, you don't watch a slide show about iPhones and iMacs. You play with them.)

I recently was working with a high-end clothing accessories manufacturer who was moving into lower end discount stores. The CEO was preparing to talk to skeptical Wall Street stock analysts with the message: "Only the price is lower; the style and quality is still top drawer!" I suggested that he bring some of their scarves and handbags. A risk-averse assistant said, "No, it's just not done." But that doesn't mean it can't or shouldn't be done! I think making samples available to see and feel helps sell on Wall Street as well as on Main Street.

## Another Visual Aid Is You!

Finally, keep in mind that your personal appearance is itself a visual tool. Your clothes send a message. Make sure that message reinforces the one you are sending with your words, your motions, and your slides, videos, or props.

One of the questions I am most frequently asked by men and women planning presentations is: "What should I wear?" My answer is, "You should look among the best in your audience."

Whatever you do, you do not want to look like an outsider. That means that you don't want to underdress, but—while you always want to appear well put together—you also do not want to overdress. Someone once said your clothes should never be more interesting than you are.

In order to dress like the best in your audience you will, of course, need to know how your audience is likely to dress. If you don't know, ask. Consider this part of your due diligence. I was working with top salespeople at a large commercial real estate firm. The culture at their firm is on the formal side, but they often sell to people who are far more casually dressed. I had to remind them that presenting externally was different from presenting internally. They needed different wardrobes for different situations.

## The Accidental Presenter

On occasion you might also be pulled into a presentation at the last minute. For these reasons, it's a smart idea to keep an extra jacket and dress shoes in your office, just in case. Along the same lines, even if your culture is business casual, avoid showing up for work in anything sloppy, stained, or torn. There is such a thing as too casual when you are in the spotlight, and you should always be prepared to shine!

One thing you never want to do is to let yourself be upstaged by your clothes. Unless you are accepting an Academy Award (and, preferably, not even then) don't address an audience wearing:

- Jangling jewelry.
- Shiny or sequined clothes.
- Fashion-forward collars.
- Clothes that are overexposing.
- Clothes with busy prints or tiny pinstripes.

It's important, too, that you are comfortable. Steer clear of tight clothes and shoes that you can only bear to stand in for five minutes. If you are uncomfortable you will lose your concentration, and your audience will experience vicarious discomfort.

## Top Tips

1. Open and close without PowerPoint—not every module should have a slide.
2. Use slides as well as other visual aids, from videos to flip charts and props, as ways to maintain audience attention.
3. Remember that you are your own visual—look among the best in the room.

# CHAPTER 12

# "That's a Good Question"

## HANDLING Q&A

If you ask the most seasoned presenters, they will say that they enjoy the question-and-answer portion of their presentation. Q&A is easier than the main bit, they'll tell you, *unless* of course they are announcing layoffs or a massive SEC investigation. Such loaded situations aside, many deem Q&A a relative breeze because:

- There's little, if any, preparatory work involved.
- They can loosen up, be themselves, and add a little spice to the fare.
- The interactive process lets them know they're connecting with the audience.

However, if you read between the lines of these rationales, what these presenters are really saying is: "Well, there isn't much I can do about Q&A so I'll just wing it."

This is risky. Q&As that are not approached with forethought can go off on a tangent. They can take up an enormous amount of time and dilute, negate, or detract from your main message. As this chapter will show, you need to anticipate the Q&A session and prepare for it as thoroughly as you prepare for the rest of your talk.

## Prepare to A the Qs!

Remember the series of questions you asked in preparing for this audience. What do they know? What do they *think* they know? What might hold them back from doing what you want? (See Figure 4.1) Ask yourself if any questions remain unanswered in your presentations. Ask what kind of pushback you'll likely get. Ask what outside competitors might say. Ask those questions of yourself in different ways and in different tones and plan your answers. But remember, the best defense is a good offence. Read on!

## Don't Just Take Questions—Ask Them

There's no doubt that soliciting questions after you speak is a credibility-enhancing strategy. Your audience understands that you are willing to be challenged, to back up what you say with more specifics, and to consider opposing points of view. That said, there is really no need for a prolonged Q&A if you've done a good job with your presentation in the first place.

A good way to make sure you are providing the answers to the questions audience members will have is to incorporate those questions into your talk in the first place. In order to do so, you can:

- Use questions to set up your message point modules ("What are some of the things we can do to increase productivity?") or to introduce proof points ("Would you like to know how much time our sales force spends filling out forms each month?").
- Ask rhetorical questions, pause, and then answer them. ("So what do you think happened when we began packaging in paper instead of plastic?" ... "I'll tell you what . . .")
- Ask the group a question that people should know the answer to and get them to respond in unison. (This works especially well in a large group, and is a great way to incorporate a signpost, such as, "We're in this to make what? All together now: '*Money and friends.*'")
- Ask questions of an individual in the group. This works especially well in a smaller audience of, say fewer than 25. It also serves to keep everyone attentive because they think they might be next, just like in high school when the history

teacher broke into your reveries by asking the kid next to you the date of the Magna Carta.

- Create a slide with multiple choice questions and then reveal the answer on the following slide after everyone's had a moment to ponder.

Incorporating questions is a great way to limit later questioning *and* to vary your presentation style, to break up your cadence, to add drama. As with any such technique, you don't want to overdo it. But nearly every presentation could benefit from the use of some of these types of questions.

Unless you are planning a truly interactive presentation and have allowed the necessary time, let the audience members know you will take questions at the end of your talk. If you stop for unsolicited questions throughout you could easily get off message and run out of time.

### Gaining a Moment to Think

Not sure how to answer a question? Asking questions of audience members is also a good way to buy yourself a minute to think about what you want to say.

Try the ricochet technique to redirect a question to another member of the audience. Or try the rebound technique, asking the same question back to your questioner. Once that person speaks, you will most likely know exactly how you want to respond.

## Facing the Tough Questions

If you are, in fact, announcing some negative developments or flat-out bad news, it's only natural that you might dread questions from your listeners. Unfortunately, some people deal with this dread by "waiting and seeing if that nasty issue comes up." This often is a mistake. It's better to be proactive and control the way you explain possible challenges rather than to wait until someone asks. I conducted a survey of equity analysts about this very topic and many said specifically that they don't like executives hiding downsides because it makes them suspicious about *more* downsides. Bringing up challenges shows that you understand push back, that you have thought about all the angles, and that you have answers. You will come off as leading, not cowering.

Once the bad news is out, there will still be inevitable questions. Questions are fine, but wild cards are not, so this is where preparation becomes imperative.

Ronald Reagan spokesman Marlin Fitzwater said that at a White House press conference one could anticipate 99 percent of the questions, no matter what the situation. You can, too. At first you might feel like there are hundreds of possible questions that could come at you in all different forms. But chances are you can bucket those questions into no more than a half-dozen categories. That is how you need to view them to gain confidence and control. The key: *Use the questions to repeat your main point modules.*

Let's take a worst-case example. Jane was announcing layoffs around the holidays. Her messages concerned past, present, and future:

1.  We have built up a workforce to meet demand that is no longer there.
2.  We now are forced to lay off 100 people (explaining why). We are doing so in a humane way (detailing the severance package).
3.  We will use the savings to build a stronger company, and hopefully be able to hire back some or all of those losing their jobs.

Jane could anticipate most of the questions she would get. They would be couched in various kinds of emotional language, but they could all be addressed by referring to her original messages. She anticipated the following:

First question: *"How can you do that at this time?"*

Answer: Reinforce message 1. Demand is no longer there.

Second question: *My wife just broke her leg, my child has chronic health issues and can't work, and now I don't have a job. What do you want me to tell them now?"*

Answer: Reinforce message 2. We are humanely ensuring continued health care and job training.

Third question: *"What is humane about getting the axe at Christmas?"*
Answer: Reinforce messages 1 and 2.

Of course you cannot sound like a broken record, but you can sound your themes. Look to your main messages—which you should have on a short list in front of you—as a roadmap for where to head for your answers to all questions.

## Don't Plant—Unless You're Gardening

During her campaign to win the Democratic nomination for president, Senator Hillary Clinton wound up in hot water for planting a question in her audience. She asked someone to ask her a question about global warming so she could offer a preplanned response. The senator later apologized. About the same time a group at the government agency, FEMA, went even further. They staged an entire fake press conference to boast about the response to California's wildfires in contrast to its much criticized performance in the wake of Hurricane Katrina. FEMA boss Michael Chertoff apologized for his employees by saying, "I think it was one of the dumbest and most inappropriate things I've seen since I've been in government."

Those cases offer lessons for the business world. Don't give in to the temptation to plant questions. In my experience it almost always looks contrived or like you can't handle what comes up naturally. If you want to raise an issue in Q&A bring it up yourself. Don't fake it.

## Handling Difficult Audience Members

Whether your news is bad news, good news, or simply informative or entertaining news, there is always the chance that you will meet with an obnoxious questioner—or perhaps more than one—during a Q&A session (or, in some cases before you even get the Q&A). All obnoxious questioners are not created equal. Different types require different strategies.

**The Confronter:** You know this type the minute you see him. He walks in with a swagger, sits back in his chair, and cocks his head in a way that says, "Hey, I don't really need to be here. Let's get this over with." Only after you deliver your presentation does he perk up. Q&A is his payday, the time when he can challenge, argue, and make life difficult.

The next time you spot him, try engaging him before the Q&A. Ask him his name early and direct one or two questions his way: "Jim, what would you have done with this?" Of course Jim might take longer than the average Joe to opine, but now you have made him an ally. You can correct any of his false assumptions and try to find common ground.

If this technique doesn't work, and your confronter insists on filibustering, try the *fairness appeal.* Tell your challenger, "I know you're really passionate about this but I want to be sensitive to the group's interests, so let's talk more afterward." Now you have made an ally of your audience. It is all of you versus the questioner.

**The Question Hog:** Even someone with relatively benign questions might insist on peppering you with loads of them, barely letting you get out one answer before wedging in a follow-up. After taking a few fast questions, try turning to your flip chart and jotting down two or three key words that reflect his questions (e.g., "proof for sales projection"). Promise you will revisit them in the course of your presentation. Charting his queries will slow him down and most often, will allow your show to go on. Do try to make good on your promise during or after your presentation.

Another way to get the stage back from a Question Hog involves the use of body language. As you answer the third or fourth question, start with your eyes on its asker, nod as if you are going to respond to him, and as you answer, move your eyes to other audience members and walk away. Move toward the rest of the group, and call on someone else to join in on the answer or call on someone else for the next question.

Question Hogs enjoy being center stage. You essentially take them off stage when you move toward others.

**The Disrupter:** The Disrupter doesn't ask you a direct question. Instead he elbows his neighbors, whispers, and snickers. You might assume it is criticism or sarcasm that he is expounding, but in truth he might be talking about something completely unrelated to your topic. Nevertheless, the disruptive effect is just the same.

This is when you *want* eye contact. Stop talking and stare straight at the Disrupter until he notices you. Then ask, "Did you have a question?" (He probably won't, or he will come up with something innocuous.)

In the event that your disrupter is so self-absorbed he fails to notice your stare, consider enlisting the help of the audience: "What can we do to get this fellow's attention?"

**The Nitpicker:** Nitpickers question every statistic and obsess on every decimal point. They always want more facts and figures. They might be perfectly well meaning, but you can get bogged down if you have all the answers they want—and you can get flustered if you don't. This is another good occasion to take things off line. Assure the questioner that his questions are valid, but because they are so specific you'd like to meet later to get to the bottom of things.

Finally, don't forget about your supporters. If you've done a good job there should be members of your audience who compliment you and who build on your message. Don't just thank them as most presenters do. Use them as an opportunity to repeat your message. For example, you can say, "Thanks, Jane, for recognizing the merits of the new incentive plan."

## The Sound of Silence

One thing presenters are typically concerned about is, what if I ask for questions and no one has any? This can make you and everyone else think that people didn't listen or that you failed, but much more likely it is because no one wants to be the first to speak. You need to get the ball rolling. Always have a few questions up your sleeve that you, in effect, can ask of yourself. For example, "You know, one of the questions I've been getting is, 'How soon we will start to add to the team?'"

Another thing you can do in situations like this is to turn the tables. Tell your audience that if they have no questions for you, you have some for them. *Poll* them as to what they thought was most important and then rank the points. This gets them talking about why. It sparks an interactive dynamic, which is a positive outcome for any presentation.

## Top Tips

1. Incorporate rhetorical questions into your presentation. Ask yourself the questions you expect from the audience. It makes your talk stronger and limits later questioning.
2. Anticipate the toughest possible questions—maybe something about which a competitor might challenge you—and look to your main message points as a roadmap for answers.
3. Use your body language to discourage difficult questioners—nod at them but then visually and physically move away from the hound who is dogging you. It takes them off stage.

# CHAPTER 13

# Sharing the Stage

## PANELS AND TEAM PRESENTATIONS

When is it better to hear a chorus than a soloist?

When the music demands range.

Just as a choir can be more engaging than an individual singer, a team or a panel can be more engaging than an individual speaker. Orchestrated properly, a shared stage is potentially a more interesting way to deliver information than having one person talk for 20 minutes straight.

Team and panel presentations, the subjects of this chapter, are becoming more and more common. This strategy makes particular sense given the short attention span of today's typical audience. Remember, with every open there is a spike in attention, and each new voice is, in effect, a new open.

There is an essential difference between team and panel presentations. In the former, you get a variety of voices sounding a unified message. In the latter, you should get not only a variety of voices but also a variety of viewpoints.

But both forums have something in common as well: The key to their success is thorough preparation.

## Team Talk: A Resonant Symphony

Team presentations can be done internally, for example at planning and budget meetings attended by multiple departments, or externally, to sell or inform. In either case, having multiple speakers working as a unit can allow you to put different areas of expertise on display, to show a depth of knowledge, and to enhance the sheer "show" value of what you are presenting.

Copresenters are like members of an orchestra who blend their instruments to craft a symphony. When they are in sync the result can be spellbinding. If one sounds a false note, everything can fall flat.

Team presenters can share great success, but they will also share failure. To ensure success you have to work together. That means not simply carving out who covers what, but understanding team members' strengths and challenges and factoring these into your planning.

I know you're thinking, "easier said than done." It's tough enough to find the time to prepare yourself, let alone orchestrate with others. However, it will be easier than you imagine if you follow these strategies:

**Designate a leader.** I recently sat down with an ambitious banker who had just joined a new firm. She and two colleagues were scheduled to present to the CEO. She had no idea what her colleagues wanted to say and was having a hard time getting them to set aside time to talk about it. It wasn't that they didn't want to do well; they just couldn't find prep time. She felt handcuffed, frustrated, and frantic. No one was in charge. I suggested that she take the reins and make assignments. That caught her copresenters' attention, and they let her take the lead.

There might be times when selecting a leader requires some negotiation, but in the end *who* the leader is not as important as the fact that the group has someone in charge of coordination. There must be a leader.

**Decide on three key message points.** I worked with a financial services presentation team consisting of the firm's CEO and the heads of the company's four business lines. All of them were extraordinarily busy. They had lined up a big press conference in New York City to explain their company's current direction. We all met the day before. Each business head had his own slides and knew basically what he wanted to say. They each had their own message points, but what was unclear was what tied them all together. They hadn't melded the *team's* top three points—points showing where they were going as a business entity and how they were different from everyone else.

When they did this their presentation became memorable. Although each speaker made his own points, they all referred back to the main themes. This reorganization also allowed the CEO to do an effective opening and closing that tied everything together and to create segues using a signpost for reinforcement.

**Play to your strengths.** Not all presenters are created equal. It's fine to allot additional time to those who present well, but not so much where others are marginalized. Weaker speakers can often do a good job of presenting factual proof modules or of introducing supporting visual material. I once worked with a team member at a pharmaceutical company who confided that he felt embarrassed by his very limited speaking role. But he was introducing powerful video—a client testimonial of a woman whose life had been saved by their new drug therapy. He was the one standing by while the audience was brought to tears. It was he who got credit by appearing moved himself and by delivering a summary line: "This is what we all work for, isn't it?"

**Work together—plan and rehearse.** Each team member must know what the others will say. Copresenters should share their key messages and their narrative thought flow at an early stage. During your planning phase make sure, too, that the look of all slides is similar. Graphics, colors, and use of space should follow through from one team member's visuals to another's. (Don't try to out-PowerPoint one another!)

Rehearse the entire presentation at least once together. When you do, pay special attention to how each of you is ending so that you create smooth transitions. (As a news anchor I always did this to create smooth segues between stories.) Rehearsal time is also a good time to discuss what is likely to come up during Q&A. Team leaders should take many questions, but not all. They should appoint designated hitters to address questions specific to their areas of expertise.

## Twos and Threes

Ideally, team presentations have three members, perhaps two. Very rarely do you want more than three speakers in the average 20- to 30-minute or even hour-long presentation. While there is great value in a variety of voices, too many can be distracting and confusing.

## Team Style, Team Spirit

With team presentations, as with individual talks, style counts for a lot. When it comes to team style, the most important thing is to show that you *are* a team. Knowing each other's content, crafting team messages, and coordinating slides are things you will do ahead of time. During your presentation, however, it's important to show you are a team by the way you relate to one another.

**Look connected:** All too often I see team members rifling through notes or examining a hangnail while another member of the team is presenting. If you aren't engaged, why should the audience be? How would it look if Josh Beckett sat in the dugout reading a novel when he wasn't on the mound? He knows that even when he is not center stage he is still part of the show.

It doesn't matter how you feel about your teammates. Whether you admire them immensely or think they're egotistical jerks, you need to stand by them. When you do so, you all win.

**Handle the handoff:** Don't just mumble, "Thanks Bob," as you slide your notes onto the podium. Make eye contact with the person who spoke before you. Consider adding a friendly or complimentary line—or underscore an interesting point Bob made, especially if you are the team leader. Remember repetition is important and if you show you have a connection, the audience will feel more connected to the team.

I was working with the CEO and CFO of a company as they prepared for a road show to raise money from investors for an initial public offering. When the CEO was done with his piece of the presentation, he planned to say simply,

"Now Luis will provide the financials." He did not feel the occasion called for an artful introduction—after all, savvy investors just want the facts. But one key fact all investors and analysts want to establish is whether a management team works well together. Knowing this, I asked the CEO if he and his colleague had known each other for long. "Oh yes," they both grinned. "We go way back. We actually worked at a Fortune 100 company together for years, and before that . . ." So, we added a line or two, including how the two men bonded during all-nighters while pulling together a fairly well-known acquisition. It took only a few seconds but it added a lot in net value. It showed that they knew and liked one another, that they worked well together, and that they have pulled off impressive accomplishments as a team.

## Teaming Up for Conference Calls

Since Regulation Fair Disclosure (RegFD), publicly owned companies have gotten used to quarterly earnings calls. These are conference calls with investors, equity analysts, and hedge fund managers (and often anyone who wants to dial in) designed to level the playing field for individual investors by ensuring that analysts don't receive information that might affect stock prices before it is publicly disclosed. More and more, these phone calls consist of team presentations, which are usually fairly boring 20-minute read alongs . . . until the Q&A begins. (One analyst told me she usually uses those recitations as a time to do her bills and only starts to listen during the Q&A.)

Sophisticated companies are trying to change this because they understand that they have more control over how the news is received if people actually listen to their presentation. One company I worked with decided to change voices a little more frequently. Rather than have the CEO read everything she had to say, followed by the CFO running through numbers, they had the CEO deliver headlines, the CFO do financials, and *then* they introduced a great new hire who talked ad strategy for just a bit before turning back to the CEO and CFO. Everytime they changed voices people tuned back in. They got great reviews for varying a staid formula.

## Panel Presentations: Mixing It Up

Unlike team presentations, which are meant to reinforce a single point of view, panels are meant to be provocative. In the true sense of that word, a good panel provokes thought and discussion—not only among the panelists but, afterward, among audience members.

Panels can be used internally or externally in any situation in which you want to offer a variety of points of view. What makes panels stimulating is that not all participants are likely to agree. In fact, for a good panel you don't *want* everyone to agree. That would defeat the whole point.

I coach a number of people who participate in nationally televised panel discussions. If you watch the gabfests of *Hardball with Chris Matthews, The McLaughlin Group,* or Gwen Ifill's slightly calmer *Washington Week* on PBS, you will see a model of what can work in a corporate setting, albeit with some modification. Participants have something to speak about and know how to speak up. They always manage to get a word in edgewise, knowing that even the most diplomatic moderator can't stop often to water a shrinking violet.

I'm obviously not suggesting that some of the more incendiary tactics employed on television shows are appropriate for, say, an automotive industry trade show. You can't shout down the first speaker on your panel ("Arnold, do you have a screw loose?!") just because it worked on *McLaughlin.* You have to adjust to your audience. But that doesn't mean you can't stir things up and bring the temperature of the room up a few degrees.

But once again, it's critical to prepare with care.

### Moderating a Panel

If you are asked to moderate a panel, think of yourself as a show producer. Identify a subject that will truly interest the audience (say, automotive fuel efficiency). Then consider various points of view on the subject (electric cars, hydrogen cars, ethanol fuel, switch grass fuel) and think about who might express them best.

Plan on amassing four or five speakers for a 60- to 90-minute panel. Select participants carefully. Engaging, dynamic personalities are as important as the depth of information. It might not be the head of the department or initiative who would make the best panelist, but rather an outspoken member of the team.

Prepare a brief introduction of each speaker and add a line indicating they'll provide interesting perspective—a kind of "stay tuned for this guy" teaser. Allow each speaker to offer a three- to five-minute opening statement and then get ready for the fireworks.

In the midst of a good panel discussion you don't know exactly what will happen. That is the intriguing part for the audience. Of course you will not know what will unfold either. Nevertheless, you need to stay in control.

- Keep track of conversation hogs and create space for those who are not aggressive (but don't come to the aid of the timid too often, especially if they're not delivering the goods when they've got the spotlight).
- Be ready to throw a lighted match into the dialogue when things get dull. If John McLaughlin asks, "If Syria actively defended Hezbollah, wouldn't the U.S. have to side with Israel?" it's bound to spark discussion.
- Avoid yes or no questions—they are dead ends.
- Listen carefully. Paraphrase or mirror big points and be able to ask smart follow-up questions.
- Protect ideas. Don't let them be attacked until articulated.
- Organize and connect content. Take notes periodically and summarize for the group: "So, now we've established that . . ."
- Maintain eye contact with all the panelists (If you don't look at them, why should the audience?) and stay alert to body language that says they're ready to speak up.

Always keep in mind that a panel is not about the moderator's opinions. Your job is to facilitate, not to perform. Your job is to be interested rather than interesting. Of course, you should be smart and professional, but don't upstage anyone. As a producer, you are answerable to the audience.

### Being a Panel Participant

If you're asked to be a panel participant, it's probably because you have a distinct point of view. Prepare to stay true to it, elaborate on it, and defend it. Take what I said about the challenges of preparing for a team presentation and multiply that for a panel. It is important that you know what your fellow presenters are going to say. But they may not be cooperative—indeed they may be competitors—so you'll need to do your due diligence. Talk to the panel coordinator and anyone else who might know your fellow panelists to find all you can about them. Find out who is in the audience and what they want to know (WIIFM). Know what the format will be (how long are opening statements, will there be an audience Q&A after the discussion?).

Now, prepare *all seven modules* on your subject. Make sure you use your headline and three provocative message points—preferably in your opening remarks—but you should also have everything else ready to roll out as needed: context, proofs, a signpost, a summary, and a call to action.

When you're in the thick of it, keep these tips in mind:

- Don't try to give a speech when asked a question. Be brief, be bright, think sound bite.
- Take brief notes when other panelists speak, especially on points with which you disagree.
- If you're having a hard time getting a word in:
  - Listen for a word or thought you can build on or contradict. For example, if Jill talked about the downward pressure on home prices, you say, "We just aren't seeing that in our market." This is best done on Jill's heels, but you can wait a bit, or use it when you are asked a question that you are less prepared to answer.
  - Use body language. Raise your hand, nod or shake your head to attract the moderator's attention.
  - Jump in with, "Another way to look at this is . . ." or, "What's really important here . . .", or—best of all—"I couldn't disagree more!" Any good moderator will take that bait.

## The Dual Audience

As a panel participant, think of yourself as having two audiences: the moderator and those watching the panel. Shape your messages for those watching but direct your responses to the moderator and other panelists. You should answer a question put to you by the moderator with your eyes on him, but in the course of your answer look out to the audience and then back to the moderator. This is a way of building audience support for you and your position.

Above all, stay engaged in the moment. No daydreaming. Even if someone else is talking, you are still on stage. And no sulking or silent treatment if a fellow panelist says something you don't like. This is no time to nurse hurt feelings. This is your show, and the show must go on.

## Top Tips

1. Designate a team leader who will open, close, and coordinate roles and team messages.
2. Find out the last point the person who precedes you will make and use this to segue smoothly into your portion of the presentation.
3. Prepare for a panel with all of your message modules; at the least, find a way to get in your headline and three key message points.

# CHAPTER 14

# A Moveable Feast

## PRESENTING TO INTERNATIONAL AUDIENCES

Americans are notorious for being ethnocentric—naive about what does and doesn't work beyond our borders. And our gaffes aren't limited to tourists sporting socks with sandals, ball caps, and fanny packs demanding loudly, "Doesn't anyone speak English here?" In addition, we've spent big ad dollars saying and doing dumb things in business.

We tried to sell canned fish in sushi-loving Japan. And we tried to sell a car called the Nova (translating as "doesn't go" in Spanish) in Central and South America, where, by the way, the dairy association's successful "Got milk?" campaign translated to, "Are you lactating?" and Frank Perdue's slogan, "It takes a strong man to make a tender chicken," came out, "It takes an aroused man to make a chicken affectionate." The hits continue on the billboards and in the boardrooms.

The good news is that executives are increasingly being asked to present to other cultures and in other countries. And there is increasing interest in doing the right things in front of the right audiences—wherever they are. This chapter is devoted to showing how that can be done.

## Know Before You Go: Ask Who, What, and How?

If you are planning an international presentation your first obligation, as always, is to find out *who* your audience will be. Whether you are speaking in Dubai, Dublin, or Detroit, find out how diverse the group is. Then find out *what* they care about. Ask what is dominating the local headlines, entertainment, and cultural scene (all potentially usable items for your opening, your anecdotes, and your proof modules).

Next, find out *how* you can best get your message across while avoiding misunderstandings or irritations. I always ask if there is anything Americans do that irks people. Recently an executive in Mexico replied that they often snicker about how Americans always try to break the ice with talk about the weather. "We never do that he said. We prefer to exchange stories about our families."

Sensitize yourself to taboos on gestures and body language as well. You know how you curl your finger to beckon someone to come closer? Well, in Hong Kong, Indonesia, and Australia this gesture is used to summon animals, or ladies of the night. As for that thumbs-up gesture, which signifies "good job" or "attaboy" in the United States, don't try it in Iran, Greece, Sardinia, or West Africa, where it is considered the foulest of hand signs. Sometimes even the most unwitting bit of body language can be misinterpreted. I know a consultant who inadvertently offended some members of a New Zealand audience when he casually leaned back against a conference table while presenting. It was explained to him later that the Maori, New Zealand's indigenous people, consider it insufferably rude for one's backside to touch a table surface.

Since many of these missteps are simply impossible to intuit, it's a good idea to consult a reliable source. There are good books on this subject, like *Gestures: The Do's and Taboos of Body language Around the World* by Roger Axtell. The U.S. Department of Commerce and embassies can also be helpful.

If you fancy yourself funny, you might want to take special care before you showcase your wit. Get the opinion of local people in your Mumbai or Shanghai office if you have a cartoon or bit of humorous banter to share. Humor is highly subjective and often culturally based. If you fail to run your jokes by someone who knows how they will translate, your intended laugh lines could be met with stony silence, or worse.

## Same Language, Different Meanings

There can be linguistic misunderstandings even between those who speak the same language. In England, for example, a "scheme" is synonymous with a "project." There's no suggestion of anything underhanded. Be sure to check your text for words that may have different connotations.

Keep in mind that the very concept of presentations differs in different cultures. While the use of PowerPoint is becoming more common abroad, slideware-based presentations tend to be very structured and direct—just like Americans. In many parts of the world, business proceeds in a less structured manner and at a slower pace. You might need to do a lot of foundational work in one-to-one settings rather than in groups. Ask first. Look before you leap.

## Tips for the Traveling Presenter

Although you will want to research each culture and audience specifically, there are some generic tips that apply universally when speaking in a foreign setting.

**Slow down:** If you are speaking English to a group that does not have English as its first language, your audience will obviously comprehend more if you proceed at a less-than-breakneck pace. If you are speaking in a language that is not your first language, slowing down will help the audience understand you despite your accent. Accents are one of the biggest concerns for those lucky enough to speak a foreign language, but don't be self-conscious about having one. Business people are becoming much more accustomed to hearing them, and having an accent will not detract from your message so long as people can take in what you're saying.

**Learn a few words of the language:** No one expects you to master a new tongue overnight. But learning a few words of greeting and thanks (Hello, I am happy to be here; thank you so much for listening.) will earn you points for being a good sport and will up your likeability. Be sure to pronounce your newfound vocabulary words correctly, or you may find yourself expressing an utterly inappropriate sentiment.

**Be cautious about pushing for decisions:** Take some extra time to consider your call to action module. If it is too strident it can backfire overseas. People in many cultures take a lot more time to make up their minds about what action they will take, and do not appreciate feeling pushed. They may give you the impression they plan to follow through when in reality they are just being polite.

**Join your hosts in other events:** Even if you avoid this sort of thing at home, when working abroad consider it part of the job to socialize. This allows you a forum to see what works and what doesn't work in terms of formal versus informal interactions, language subtleties, and humor.

---

### Don't Get Your Back Up

Don't let your ego trip you up. People in other cultures may show approval in what Americans consider unusual ways. In Japan, for example, it is common for people to close their eyes to concentrate on what you are saying.

---

**Understand time sense in different cultures:** I worked with a large international group of physicians about the importance of brevity. One doctor from India told me that shortening his presentation would be fine in the U.S. but that at home if you limited yourself to a crisp 20 minutes, your audience would assume you had no more to say. He needed to have a short and a longer version of his talk at the ready.

Along these lines, be aware that some cultures are averse to "saving time" by combining meals with business presentations. In the United States, we might schedule a working lunch where people grab a buffet plate and eat while speakers plow ahead with the agenda *du jour*. Don't even consider this in an Arab country, where meals are accompanied by prayer, not PowerPoint.

**Pay your respects:** I worked with a Chinese national working for a U.S. trade group. She was preparing a presentation in her native China and had a lengthy list of thank you's, acknowledging every dignitary and near dignitary in the audience. I usually try to shorten this kind of thing dramatically, advising speakers to make a quick blanket thank you statement. But in China it is very important to recognize virtually everyone in a position of influence.

**Listen carefully to Q&A:** Before you answer questions from audience members, paraphrase them and verify the gist of the query with your questioner. This ensures that you understand what is being asked of you before you respond.

Finally, keep in mind that we are all operating in an increasingly globalized business environment. Even long-entrenched cultural habits and preferences are subject to change as more people from more countries interact on a regular basis—and as the Internet continues to wield its influence. I recently worked with a German client who resisted my direction to smile and lighten up a bit. She insisted that Germans did not embrace a "smiley" approach—that they saw themselves as "serious people talking to serious people." Yet, the German technology company for which she works has lately been losing market share to companies that do not have better technology but do have better marketing and communication. The times they are a changin' and, in the end, a little adaptation may go a long way.

---

## Top Tips

1. Learn about the culture and country where you'll be speaking. Ask in advance if there are mistakes Americans commonly make—then don't make them.
2. Learn a few lines in your host country's language, and speak slowly.
3. Be aware of time sense in different cultures—have shorter and longer versions of your talk ready.

# PART

# IV

# MANAGING YOUR MEDIA MOMENT

# 15

# Reporters and Those They Report To

As mentioned throughout the book, your audience is always the first thing you want to think about when you are preparing to speak. And preparing to speak to the media is no exception. But if you want to develop strong media messages, take control of the questions you are asked, *and* take control of your nerves, you must remember that when you speak to the media you are really addressing two target audiences. The first is the reporter you are facing; the second is the people whom *they* will reach—that is, your audience of stakeholders, employees, customers, and potential clients. This chapter will tell you how to deal with both parts of your audience.

## Remember Who's Watching, Remember Who's Reading

Neglecting the dual audience factor is one of the biggest mistakes people make when communicating to the media. They tend to focus on the reporter only. If the reporter is abrasive or confrontational, they respond in kind (or *un*kind, as it were). To illustrate this contention, I often use a video clip in my media training sessions that shows the legendary Exxon CEO in a CBS interview after the Valdez, Alaska, oil spill disaster. In his role as poster child for bad crisis management, this chief executive got involved in a drawn out debate with a reporter *on a live broadcast* about how often he appeared on TV. Even if the reporter was wrong or made the CEO feel like a target, debating was not a good use of his media time, and he looked like a hothead. Had he thought about who was watching—people who filled their tanks with his product, who invested in Exxon, or worked for the company—he might have taken the opportunity to speak to them directly from the heart. Rather than looking and sounding belligerent, he could have said how he felt badly about the problem. Rather than sounding like he was sweating the small stuff, he should have talked about how he was determined to become part of the solution, how Exxon had become one of Alaska's biggest employers in the cleanup effort. Regular people understand that accidents happen even if the reporter seems intent on rubbing your nose in it.

If you remember your true *intended* audience, you are more likely to keep your game face. Moreover, if you think about your target audience your messages will be better crafted and more strategic.

For example, I was working with some restaurant executives who were planning on sprucing up one of their chains. In a press interview, right off the bat they started talking about how consumers told them they wanted the restaurants to look better and deliver better service—a good story. But one of the audiences the executives wanted to reach through the media was their franchisees who, by the way, would have to foot much of the bill for the improvements in a down market. When they thought about reaching this particular audience *through* the media, they beefed up their proof module with a survey of key franchisees that said they supported efforts to upgrade certain restaurants because they hurt the brand. (If people get poor service at Restaurant A in Cleveland they don't want to eat at the Restaurant A in Oklahoma City.) Including this proof was important to show that the company was responding to *all* their constituencies. It was also good for business reporters who wanted to gauge the likelihood of the initiative's success.

## Reporters Are Different

Although reporters are not your sole audience, their needs must also be served. This is critical, because you will not be able to get your message out *through* the press unless you manage your rapport *with* the press. That means understanding reporters. So, what are reporters like, anyway? What motivates them? What interests them? You need the answers to these questions in order to get press coverage to work for you.

Reporters are different creatures. I can say this with confidence because I was a reporter for more than 20 years, first briefly in newspapers and for many years in television.

What reporters prize is nothing like what is prized in the corporate world. Corporate executives prize teamwork, uniformity, singing from the same song sheet, following the rules. They are protective about what they have worked for and created and are, in many cases, at least somewhat conservative. They'd rather live with the devil they know and by the motto that if things ain't broke they don't want to fix 'em.

Reporters, on the other hand, are scofflaws. They love challenging the status quo; they embrace change. They are always looking out for the little guy (there are more of them than there are executives or politicians). They are plain talking (so everyone can understand them). Moreover, they are more inclined to be competitive than to be team players because they are often pitted against the reporter in the next cubicle—not to mention every other media outlet in town.

As an effective communicator, it is important to understand reporters' traits because they may guide how you interact with the press. Remember, if you can't make the most of your encounter with your first audience, the press, you won't get to spread your message to your second target audience—the one you really care about.

With all this in mind, let's look at some typical reporter traits and how you can use each to your advantage.

### Curious/Suspicious

Anyone inclined to take a press release at face value is not a reporter—or at least not much of one. Reporters like to dig deeper, sniff around, and get the *real* story—the one they are hoping the competition will not get. This tendency to dig deeper can apply to any story, even to one that is ostensibly a "feel good" story. Let's say a reporter is invited to an event that celebrates foster children being permanently adopted into homes and becoming a part of a family again. If they simply go along with the press release they'll have a nice story. But many will dig deeper, perhaps focusing on just one teenager to get a story about the pain of moving from home to home and the ineptitude of the system. To the reporter's way of thinking, using this example can influence the system and create a better understanding of the issue. It's also a better story.

*Your takeaway:* When preparing for your media moment, remember that reporters are tough to control. What you serve up as a story may be just a jumping off point to them. Know that if you invite them in to talk to the CEO they may also talk to your receptionist and mailroom clerk—and in a crisis their information is just as credible, if not more so, than an executive's. That means you have to prepare *everyone* to be asked anything.

The good news—at least for noncrisis situations—is that you might curry favor with select reporters if you suggest new and different angles they can take.

### Audacious Questioners

Reporters are willing to ask anything of anyone. This is the one quality I would mention right off the bat to anyone who wanted to know what it takes to become a good reporter. They have to be the one willing to stand up in a huge lecture hall filled with awestruck audience members and ask a question of a Nobel Prize winner—even if they think it might be a dumb question.

### Can They Say That?

I once worked with a top executive who'd just won a very big salary at a young age. As part of the training exercise, I asked him why he deserved it and how he justified it. He pulled his microphone off, turned to his public relations person and demanded, "They can't ask me that, can they?" The public relations person said, "Yes they can, and they will." In order to prepare the executive for these types of questions, we worked on a message that spoke to the value the firm placed on restoring public confidence, a big job in that environment. It worked. He felt great and used it often, not just with the press.

*Your takeaway:* This audacious quality can be seen as irritating and disrespectful—even obnoxious. But like it or not, you have to prepare for it by being prepared with a host of answers for the various questions a reporter may ask. Although you don't need to answer every question (see Chapter 17 for more on handling a reporter's questions), you must expect anything, and keep your game face on when they ask a seemingly unrelated or controversial question.

### Plain Folks and Populists

Reporters wield power disproportionate to their incomes, so it is easy to forget how they live their lives and where they come from. Although there are some media stars who make millions, they are rare, and their salaries don't approach the mega-millions of some of their interview subjects. The wealthy are a favorite target for the press because people always like to hear about lifestyles of the rich and famous—especially when there is occasion to show that their lives can be miserable, too.

Keep in mind also that the vast majority of people that comprise a reporter's audience are not wealthy. Even members of a distinct business audience, such as the *Wall Street Journal* readership, are not as well off as most of the executives the paper features.

*Your takeaway:* Adjust what you say and how you say it. In my training sessions I often tell clients that reporters get along better with the folks in the subway than the folks in the boardroom. So be the guy in the neighborhood: loosen up a bit and laugh. Be informal—but not obsequious. Aim for the conversational but cautious tone you would use with a boss you don't know well.

### Good at Getting You Comfortable

To be a good reporter you have to know how to get people comfortable, and subtly get them to let down their guard. To get at the truth, reporters are great with flattering and joshing. They usually have all the qualities that make a great salesperson.

*Your takeaway:* Don't let your guard down. Be friendly but know that reporters aren't your friends. On the other hand, they are not your enemies. They are not out to get you; they are out to get a story. That is their top priority.

## Did I Say That?

Shortly after Ben Bernanke became chairman of the Federal Reserve, he publicly admitted to a "lapse of judgment" in telling Maria Bartiromo, an attractive television business reporter he chatted with at a banquet, that investors had "misunderstood" his comments about interest rates. Bartiromo tweaked the story, saying Mr. Bernanke "had surprising comments," which in turn set off a round of nail biting in financial markets. After this incident, there was widespread speculation that the new Fed chairman was about to become a much less interesting party guest. (He had become wiser in the ways of reporters.)

### Slippery

Reporters may not show you *all* their cards. For example, they'll tell a pet store owner they would like to do a story on cute puppies when they are investigating puppy mills. They'll tell a source they work for a think tank when they are also a freelancer who contributes to newspapers and publishes a blog.

*Your takeaway:* Ask yourself if the story the reporters says he is doing is a viable story. Is it news? Does it make sense? If you are unsure then ask him what specifically prompted his interest. Ask, too, for *all* the places the story might appear.

## Beware the Blogosphere

Before you reveal sensitive information to a stranger these days, you have to know if they write anywhere for anyone—and that includes writing blogs. These days more and more reporters get their stories from blogs. I was recently at a dinner talking with a top-tier technology reporter who said she gets most of her stories from blogs. I happened to sit next to the international editor for a big weekly magazine who said blogs inform or are a voice in many stories. Blogs count. They have become a primary source for reporters.

### Quick, Intelligent Generalists

While reporters tend to be quicker than average, they are not geniuses, nor are most truly specialists. One of their core competencies is the ability to gather a lot of complex information, synthesize, and summarize it. True, many business or medical reporters have more knowledge of their subjects than most reporters, but they still may not have deep knowledge. Regardless, all reporters are good at sounding like they know more than they do.

*Your takeaway:* Before you talk to a reporter, do a Google search on the topic of the story. See what is out there. You don't have to read the whole story (neither do most reporters), but this will give you a heads-up about possible questions. Additionally, doing this will help you sound smarter and make your messages resonate better.

If you consider yourself an expert on your subject, you may scoff at the idea of doing homework on it. But I can't stress strongly enough that in addition to knowing your topic, it is also necessary to know what the press has recently covered. Don't overdo it. If you are talking about, say, manufacturing concerns in China, you don't need to go to China to do your homework, but do know what other companies with plants in China are saying.

You can also ask reporters to e-mail a few of their questions to you in advance. You don't want to come off as suspicious, but in truth this will help you craft the message you want to get out. It's best not to answer questions off the cuff. You don't want to lose a good press coverage opportunity, but see if you can buy a little prep time by saying you have to attend a quick meeting or take a call first. Use the time to do your search and to plan what you do and don't want to say.

## Research Your Reporter

Although I've just listed traits most reporters have in common, it is important that you know about the individual reporter to whom you will be talking. A good reporter will do some research on you before speaking with you. You need to turn the tables and do the same.

First, get the name of the reporter who is coming to see you and do a search in the publication she writes for (or watch her show if she is on television). Then, see what stories she has done, because that gives you an idea of what kinds of stories she will do in the future. While reviewing her work, carefully pay attention to the style of reporting, for example, is she a "gotcha" guy or more of a flattering feature writer? If the writer has reported on your subject before, what is her take on it? What is her focus? Lastly, don't forget to check out all the publications, blogs or shows she reports for.

## No Press Bashing, Please

I know it's easy to bash the press.

Many say, "They only report bad news," but, after all, a plane landing safely is not news.

Many say, "They want controversy," but that is a good thing because it means they will seek out both sides of a story.

We say, "They are out to get people," but the people who are tripped up by the press are usually tripping over their own words.

If you are prepared and follow the suggestions that I have provided within this chapter, then you are not likely to get burned when you convey your message during your media moment.

Remember, the reality of the news business today is that reporters are always under the gun to file stories to fill the 24/7 news cycle. As such, they appreciate sources that make their jobs easier so be clear, be engaging, and be knowledgeable.

### Top Tips

1. Although you're looking at a reporter, don't forget to talk to your other audience as well: address your employees, clients, potential customers, the stakeholders you really want to reach.
2. Be friendly, but remember reporters are not your friends (they are not out to get you, but they *are* out to get a story).
3. Always ask who a reporter works for and get the whole story. Does the reporter contribute to other shows or publications? Does he write a blog?

# CHAPTER 16

# Making Your Message the Story

I spend a lot of my time assuring executives that talking to the media is a more credible and cheaper way to get their message out than is advertising. But for media exposure to be effective, you must take responsibility for managing what comes out of your mouth. Achieving control takes the right preparation. Of the thousands of clients I've worked with, most begin making mistakes before the tape recorder starts rolling. They either prepare for their media moment in the wrong way or they don't prepare at all. This chapter will help you avoid both pitfalls and show you how to get set for media in ways that make sense.

## The Wrong and Winding Road to Media Prep

The wrong way to prepare for a media interview is to start with, "What are they gonna ask me?" rather than, "What do I want to say?" As discussed in Chapter 12, this is akin to asking, "What slides do we have?" as a starting point for presentations. It's an approach in which you relinquish control.

Specifically, if you first ask yourself, "What are they gonna ask me?" you put yourself in a reactive state of mind right off. It's as if you are in a batting cage trying to hit every ball tossed your way, rather than pitching a few balls of your own. You need to view an interview as an opportunity to pitch your ideas, to offer your point of view on the topic the press is covering—even when the topic is your troubles.

So, first things first: Start your media prep by thinking about what you want to say to *your* audience. Then brainstorm tough questions. This approach will help you beef up your messages in a proactive way.

If you have a public relations team that wants to support you in your media appearances, you can count yourself as fortunate in the sense that they won't let you go in cold. However, if your PR team shows up with a ream of papers listing every possible question you could be asked with a corresponding answer, beware. You won't have time to read, let alone memorize, all of that. And even if you could, it would not be the most effective way to get ready. Tell your team you want to focus on your story first.

### Don't Go When You Don't Know

Another common mistake is to go into a media interview cold. It's easy to rationalize this by saying you don't have any time to prepare and that besides, "no one knows more than I do on this subject." But you need to keep in mind that being an expert does not necessarily make you a good speaker who can clearly articulate your key points during an interview. Therefore, it's important to find the time to prepare for your interview. Begin by boiling down your message so that you can get to the essence of your point. In order to prevent your reporter from getting bored or going off on a tangent, try to get your strongest points in there and get them in there fast. A reporter is most open to listening early in an interview.

## Go in Cold, Land in Hot Water

No matter how tempting it is to get a little free publicity, you have to know what you're getting into. An author friend of mine went on the Jerry Springer show to promote a book when the show was new and she had never seen or even heard of it. It turned out the host and the audience, egged on by that host, had a bone to pick with her point of view—the good parenting required listening skills—which she felt was badly misrepresented. Too bad it was too late to do much about it. She had to take a lot of flak without achieving the goal of promoting her book. Later, she joked with me that she felt lucky to get out alive, but that's not really all you want from a media interview, is it?

## The Right Prep, the ROI Prep

When you prepare the right way for a (ROI) interview you *will* achieve a better return on your investment of time and effort, and you will mitigate risk. The right preparation for media is not very different from the right preparation for planning a presentation. (In fact, it might help you to view a media interview as a presentation that feels like a conversation and that will be punctuated by questions.) In both cases, you can use your modules as your anchor.

Having flexible message modules at your disposal will help you to do what reporters love—sound prepared without sounding rehearsed. I stress sounding unrehearsed because the last thing any reporter wants is for you to monopolize the conversation and make a speech. If you do that, the reporter is likely to shut off the tape recorder and say thanks, but no thanks. On the other hand, reporters appreciate a prepared interview subject. A friend of mine, a veteran *60 Minutes* producer who travels all over the world collecting interviews for the premier investigative newscast, told me that, in general, if someone is prepared they'll get a better interview. Bill O'Reilly told me once he won't have anyone on his show unless the guest knows how to deliver and how to cope with his style.

So, take the advice from the experts and use your modules to get ready. They will allow you to put your best foot forward, not in your mouth.

## Modules for Media

Chapter 2 introduced seven modules for preparing outstanding presentations. These modules are:

1. *Headline:* tell them what you'll tell them.
2. *Context:* a bit of background information.
3. *Three Message Points:* a trio of statements that flesh out your headline.
4. *Proofs:* facts, analogies, and anecdotes that illustrate your points.
5. *Signpost:* a brief, catchy ongoing refrain.
6. *Summary:* tell them what you've told them.
7. *Call to Action:* say what you want them to do.

For media, the module list is pretty much the same, with just a few minor tweaks. Signposts and calls to action, while effective in presentations for rallying the troops and getting potential investors excited, usually don't fit in when speaking to a reporter. They will make you sound as if you are speechifying. But the remaining five modules should still be your guides. The media modules are:

1. Headline
2. Context
3. Three Message Points
4. Proofs
   a. Fortify with fact
   b. Add analogies
   c. Add anecdotes
5. Summary

As we look at these in detail, be sure to keep one thing in mind: Whenever the press is involved, let the guiding mantra that shapes your modules be *what's new? what's new? what's new?* To a reporter, the *new* is what makes the *news*.

### The Headline: Keep It Simple

The best way to come up with a headline module for media is to literally envision the headline of the reporter's story just as you would write it. What do you want the story to focus on? If you're not certain, ask yourself:

- Of all the facts and ideas, what one thing most interests *you?*
- Of all your facts and ideas, which one *surprises, amuses,* or *represents change?*
- What message do you want to leave 'em with?

Sometimes my clients insist they have nothing substantially new to offer. But when pressed they will say, "Oh, well, we do have news but it was in our press release." But don't assume the reporter read the press release, or read it carefully (especially if it was more than one page). And even if the reporter did read it, you can freshen that news with an up-to-the-minute development.

Another objection I hear is, "I don't know if anyone's heard our news about X, but I'm already busy with Y." It's understandable that something may not feel new to you if you've moved on to planning the next new thing, but if the press and public do not yet know about something, it's news to them.

One more objection to framing a news-oriented headline is, "Our competition is saying the same thing." My reply is that everyone may be singing the same song, but you need to sing it best. The right way to do this is to deliver your headline in a simple manner. How simple is simple?

- Test it on a fifth grader or, if it involves technology, test it on your mother.
- Be specific—don't use amorphous, tired words like "solutions."
- Be real—don't use euphemisms. If it quacks like a duck it's a duck; if it's a faster, smarter duck, say so.

Remember, a headline is short and is meant to fit across a few newspaper columns. If you're going on television, keep it shorter and simpler still. The small screen isn't a place for big thoughts.

## Headline Helpers

Reporters love controversy and conflict. Think about that when you are developing headline messages. Can your frame your message in terms of a challenge to the status quo?

Reporters also like tips and advice. Can you pass along a piece of insider know-how? For example, if you create educational software, what advice might you give to the mother of a precocious toddler? If you work for the chamber of commerce, what advice or tips might you provide to someone moving into town?

### Context: Keep It Brief

Context offers a brief glimpse of background, often touching on surrounding circumstances and time frames. ("We've been importing goods from Mexico since the inception of NAFTA." "We've been trying to come up with a feasible hydrogen car for 10 years.") If you like, you can e-mail a bit of context to a reporter ahead of time. But whatever you do, avoid the temptation to spend an hour educating a member of the press as you will come off as arrogant and will bore the reporter.

I can't count the times clients have said, "We spent so much time with that guy and got nothing—no quotes, no attribution. We thought we were a shoe-in for this piece."*Wrong.* Reporters owe you nothing, no matter how long you talk with them or how much information and insight you give them. If you want to be quoted, you have to earn it by saying something quotable.

### Three Message Points and Proofs: Dress Them Up Before You Take Them Out

The question I'm most often asked in media training is, "How do I get quoted?" Clients are always curious about what makes a good quote, and why reporters for different papers and newscasts will so often latch onto exactly the same quote. As such, I always tell clients that the best way to get quoted is to dress up their message points and proofs.

As always, remember the power of threes. You should support your headline with three message points. As a general guideline for coming up with these points, think of the three Ps:

1. *People:* what you and your employees are doing.
2. *Products:* what you have to offer.
3. *Plans:* what will happen next.

Once you've come up with three strong points and proofs to support them, you have to dress these modules up so they are quotable. In order to do so, you should:

- Omit anything vague.
- Use vivid language.
- Use your sense of humor.
- Use surprising twists in language (perhaps remixing a common aphorism . . . such as, "out of mind, out of sight").
- Let your reactions be personal and emotional.

Recently, I copied all of the quotes out of three consecutive days of the *Wall Street Journal* and bucketed them into three groups: factual, colorful, and emotional.

Emotional quotes were in the majority, followed narrowly by colorful ones. The factual bucket was most empty because reporters don't need to quote you when they can offer a general synopsis.

When you are imparting facts, think of clever ways to say them ("We will ensure that the Hotel A you find at exit 10 is as great as the one you found at exit 1," versus "Guests will find a uniform experience at all of our facilities."). Whenever possible, couple your facts with your analogies and anecdotes, as the latter two modules allow more cleverness, creativity, and passion to come through.

### "Emotional" Doesn't Mean "Sappy"

Giving an emotional quote isn't about being a sob sister; it is about putting the *you* in your message. Rather than stating what your consumer survey showed, say, "I was surprised to find that people care more about the basics than the bells and whistles by a margin of . . ." Make sure you really act surprised or shocked when you utter that statement: Don't just say it, mean it.

I was working with an executive team busy reenergizing a brand that had become dog-eared. The brand had been a memorable part of their childhoods, but none of them were saying so. Once they did, they were quotable.

### *The Summary: Soooo . . . Anything Else?*

Often reporters, especially newspaper reporters, will ask off-handedly at the end of an interview, "Soooo, do you have anything else?" Most interviewees will say, "Noooo, I think that's about it." That's a mistake.

Take such an opportunity to summarize. Say, "I think the main things people need to understand are . . ." and recap your three message points. Even if the reporter doesn't ask if you have anything else, offer it. Say, "Well, thanks for calling, Jim. I just think it's important that people know . . ."

People often complain about reporters not getting it or not getting it right. If you summarize, you've done your best to make sure they do.

## Media Question Control: Softballs

*After* you have developed your media modules and proofs, you need to brainstorm the likeliest questions you might be asked—even the tough or dirty, rotten ones. But keep in mind that most reporters will start with a couple of softballs. Answering easy questions can be an opportunity for you to reinforce your modules if you use a few simple strategies.

1. **Flag your messages:** Begin your responses, "Here is what you need to know . . ." or "Here's what I think is important . . ."
2. **Be natural and genuine:** It's a conversation, not a quiz or speech.
3. **Think in bullets:** Limit the time spent on each answer; stop when you have said what you want to say.
4. **Say what you *can* say:** Be as forthcoming as possible; remember that "no comment" is a comment.
5. **Avoid bashing the competition:** Talk about you, not them.

Sometimes a reporter will ask multiple questions at once. ("Won't the cost of this gadget be high? Will consumers be able to justify it? Won't they want a cheaper alternative?") It's easy to get flustered when a barrage occurs. The trick is: Pick the question you want to address and tackle only that one question. ("The cost is easily justified when you consider how much energy the product will save over time.") If the reporter really wants the answer to questions you've left out, he'll ask again.

## Media Question Control: Hardballs

Now, for the hardballs. One of the most common mistakes in media training is when trainers advise clients to simply ignore difficult questions. You see this all the time in television interviews. You even see it in presidential debates: Someone is asked one thing and gives an answer that is a complete disconnect. For example:

Q: Will you or won't you raise taxes?

A: The American people are a caring people. Their hearts are big and they are concerned for the welfare of their fellow citizens.

Say what?

The person answering comes off as completely disingenuous (even smarmy), and the person watching can't help but felt irritated (even insulted). True, some very renowned people had a standing policy of arriving at an interview or press conference with absolutely no intention of actually responding to questions. Henry Kissinger, for example, subscribed to the strategy of Charles DeGaulle, who addressed reporters at the beginning of a press conference by saying, "Gentlemen, I am ready for the questions to my answers." But emulating this manner won't win you any friends—either among reporters or among the audience you really want to influence.

Therefore, I suggest that you prepare to face the music and dance. You will have to take some tough questions, but even hardball questions can offer an opportunity for you to make your points, provided you follow these guidelines.

**Correct misunderstandings:** If the question is based on an erroneous assumption, say so. Explain the facts calmly and non-defensively. That in itself is your answer.

**Find common ground:** If you've ever sold anything—or bought anything—you know the main rule of Sales 101 is "find common ground." This applies when you are selling your message. Don't swim upstream. If your company is genuinely in a profits slump and a reporter brings this up, it makes no sense to bristle or deny it. Say, "Sure, we could be doing better . . ." Now you have found a way to agree that still leaves you a chance to get to a point you want to make.

**Reframe questions:** If you are asked a question that contains negative language, don't repeat it, reframe it.

It is human nature to repeat questions. In fact, business schools tell you to mirror language even if it is negative, because it says, "I hear you," even if you disagree. Do *not* do this with a reporter because they often ask combative, "Are you still beating your wife" questions to catch you off guard and prompt a big reaction. If you repeat, "I am *not* still beating my wife . . ." their language becomes part of *your* quote. Instead, reframe the question. Say, "You are asking me about my relationship with my wife . . ." Doing this also buys you time to think.

**Bridge to your messages:** Bridging is probably the most celebrated technique for handling tough questions. It is also the most misunderstood.

Bridging involves taking a reporter's question and using it as a springboard to what you want to say. Done artfully, this is a useful technique. But done clumsily, too frequently, or too soon into the interview, it comes off as a dodge.

If your modules are well developed, then 99 percent of the time you will be able to bridge back to those messages and land in positive territory. But don't be in too much of a rush. If it's a legitimate query, answer one or two questions briefly—even if those questions are not especially what you want to talk about—before you start trying to *appropriately* cross a bridge to your primary message. Then, create a segue with a line like: "What folks may not realize is . . ." or "The fundamental issue is . . ." Or, more artfully, latch onto a word or thought that the reporter has just articulated and use *it* to bridge.

For example, a Citigroup executive was booked on CNBC the same day that her former boss, John Reed, was named to head the New York Stock Exchange. Reed's new job would be to rehabilitate the exchange, which had been in the headlines for overpaying its leader, along with a number of other hot issues. The Citigroup executive had agreed to do an interview with Maria Bartiromo to talk about a new loan program, but the big news that morning was Reed and that was what Bartiromo led with. "So," she asked her interviewee, "can Reed do the job?" The interviewee liked her former boss, but she wanted to talk about her loan program, so she briefly answered two queries about Reed and then she bridged saying, "Speaking about John's commitment to the community, it seems fitting that today we are announcing our multimillion dollar loan program to public housing." Bartiromo followed along. She crossed the bridge because she had gotten what she wanted and now could let the interviewee get what *she* wanted.

Notice the implicit *quid pro quo* here. It's not smart to simply ignore questions on topics other than your prime messages. Don't say, "Well, what I am really here to talk about is . . ." That is swimming upstream. Reporters will just turn around and say, "Well, what *I* am here to talk about is . . ." and you cannot win if they have the last say.

Figure 16.1 shows the form I use to help people bridge from tough or nasty questions to their messages. On the diagonal lines I have people list all the challenges and then brainstorm how to bridge, or move back on message.

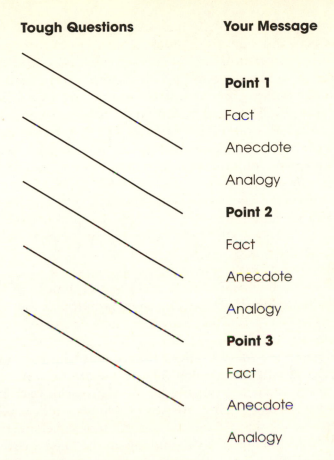

**Tough Questions**                    **Your Message**

**Point 1**

Fact

Anecdote

Analogy

**Point 2**

Fact

Anecdote

Analogy

**Point 3**

Fact

Anecdote

Analogy

**Figure 16.1    Bridge to Your Messages**

Now remember, you can't force reporters to cross your bridge. They have to want to do so, and they won't want to unless you have answered legitimate questions that are part of their agenda. Think of effective bridging as pure behavioral training, the kind you'd use to get a horse to go where you want it to go. You have to give it a tasty morsel and then move it in the direction you want, otherwise it is back to the stable.

## Handling the Ambush

As prepared as you are, there may be times when a reporter will confront you with something unsettling or even shocking that you genuinely have no knowledge of. This kind of ambush might come from a reporter you trust. It might also be sandwiched between other perfectly innocuous questions: "How are new procedures to improve your widgets working?" leads to, "We understand that government inspectors have found problems with your widgets", which in turn leads to a benign ending like, "So, you are hoping that your new procedures will address these issues?" Reporters may do this so they can say goodbye in a less sour way, but you could still be left bewildered and wondering whether or not you said the right thing.

No matter who ambushes you or how they do it, you should follow the same two rules.

1. Don't get defensive.
2. Express care, concern and commitment, but not necessarily responsibility.

I can't count how many times, as a reporter, that I was sent out with a shred of evidence to see if someone would take the bait, own up, and legitimize a slim suspicion. Sometimes they did. *But you should know better*. If a reporter shows you something that you have not seen before say you will check into it, that you'll see what the company policy and say that you will get back to him. In my training I use a clip of an investigative TV news program that shows an executive for a major chain of big box discount stores being interviewed by an investigative reporter. The reporter asks the executive about his company's use of child labor. The executive says they don't use child labor, and then the reporter starts pulling pieces of evidence out one by one—first a picture, then a video, then a shirt that he says is sold at that chain of stores. The executive is so flustered at this point that he does not even think to check whether the shirt is actually sold at his stores (it might have been, but he did not know that). But the worst part was the executive's style. Backed into a corner, he became flip. His last line—the one his audience was left with—was, "Well, terrible things happen all over the world." That answer itself was terrible. He looked like he didn't care.

Now, just because I am ending this chapter with advice for an ambush, don't assume that it is likely to happen. In the vast majority of cases, press interviews are not that eventful. Most topics don't merit crack investigation and, for better or worse, most reporters these days don't have time to do it. Remember, with a virtually endless news hole to fill, most members of the press are happy most of the time if they are given a short, solid message with something new and a catchy "hook." Serve your message that way and you'll do fine—especially if, as the next chapter explains, you serve it up with style.

## Top Tips

1. Always prepare—going in cold could leave 'em cold or land you in hot water.
2. First ask yourself, "What do I want to say?" rather than "What will they ask me?"
3. Don't be afraid to say how you feel about your subject—emotion is quotable.

# CHAPTER 17

# Serve It with Spice

Remember the importance of style when delivering a persuasive presentation? The same holds true when speaking to the press. Even a message that is new, interesting, and important can easily be buried with a dull or monotonous delivery. On the other hand, the right body language, tone, and cadence can help you make your points and ensure that what you want to say gets heard. In this chapter, you'll learn how to serve your media message in the most appetizing manner.

Serving up your media message with spice can:

- Help you get press because enthusiastic, entertaining people are in demand.
- Build your credibility because you will be better able to convince and impress.
- Help you get quoted more because you will talk plainly and be jargon-free.
- "Dull the sword," that is, help control the fallout from tough questions and questioners because you will appear natural and nondefensive.

But don't take this to mean that you should go in prepared to bring the house down with a pack of one-liners and a "let it all hang out" demeanor. There is a happy medium between baring all, on the one extreme, and speaking in humorless, clipped talking points, which some interviewees manage to do even if their topic is the upcoming school bake sale. Finding the right delivery style means finding what is comfortable for you, and remembering that moderation is a good policy in all things.

## Loosen Up, Lighten Up

If you think beyond your immediate audience (a reporter) to your ultimate intended audience (customers, investors, employees), it should be easy to understand why a wooden approach or a high-strung nervous delivery won't do. No one wants to do business with a stiff, let alone with a nervous wreck. In this section, I discuss a number of things you can do to ensure that you come across in a comfortable, casual manner.

### Project Energy, Gesture, and Smile

Style is what allows you to better control what reporters write and what sound bites they select. That is because the right style conveys energy and enthusiasm.

Take the most mundane of lines, for example: "The sky is blue." Repeat this line aloud in a flat voice and it *sounds* mundane. But if you were to practice that line every day, reading it with drama, stressing different words, slowing down, adding a sweep of the hand, raising and lowering your voice, then "the sky is blue" would sound amazingly memorable. Same content; different style; different message.

The best way to make sure that you project energy, gesture, and smile is to practice, practice, practice. Practice energizing your messages by varying the cadence and pace of your delivery. Smile (unless the news is grim) and move your hands. I urge clients to gesture even if on the phone because it is easier to emphasize the messages and quotes you want the reporter to use. I can also tell you for a fact that many CEOs stand up during phone interviews because they know this makes their voice sound crisper and more enthusiastic.

Also, avoid reading from an already prepared script or cheat sheet. Reading aloud from prepared notes is never the way to approach a media interview. It dampens your energy and limits your ability to flash your smile.

Reading can also undermine credibility. A case in point: I was sitting in an express breakfast room at a hotel in Missouri with everyone there watching CNN. A live report came on: A couple suspected in the disappearance of their three-year-old daughter during a vacation had just arrived back home. The press was waiting. Balancing another child in his left arm, the father reached into his pocket and pulled out a statement, which he read. From the other side of the breakfast room, a large man with a southern accent called out, "If you gotta read it, you got a problem." A chorus of strangers sounded a collective "ummm hmmm."

## Give 'Em Time to Get It Down

If you've said something especially strong and quotable and the reporter seems to be buying it, pause for a moment. If you're on TV give viewers a moment to let it sink in. If you're talking to a print reporter, they need time to write it down. Make sure they are scribbling. On the phone you can hear the "click, click" of the keyboard.

### Jettison the Jargon

Plain talking is extremely important to reporters. Using jargon is one of the best ways to ensure that you won't be quoted or will be mischaracterized. Jargon actually forces reporters to paraphrase, and they may get it wrong. Why not focus on doing the job for them and minimizing your risk?

Using jargon alienates not just reporters but your *real* audience. If they can't understand you, it makes them wonder if *you* understand *them*.

In an earlier chapter I mentioned the former CEO of Home Depot mishandling a television interview by continually talking about the chain's "resets"—internal jargon for "moving stuff around so people can find and reach it better." The interviewer did not know what resets were, and you can bet potential Home Depot shoppers didn't either. But any weekend handyman would have liked to know he could easily find a glue gun or a furnace filter at this do-it-yourself emporium.

Not long ago, a client of mine worried that people might think her inarticulate if she used words like "things" or "stuff." But such words are, literally, the stuff of daily conversation. Using ordinary terms doesn't make you seem ordinary; it just makes you seem accessible and understandable. You don't have to use slang, but you do have to be able to explain strategies or ideas in simple and specific ways.

### Stay Natural, No Matter What

Some interviewees are well able to maintain a casual, conversational style until a tough question comes along. Then they undergo a massive change in demeanor. Sometimes they are so taken aback that they actually recoil from the reporter. Sometimes they change their tone. Sometimes they resort to monosyllables.

Instead, just keep on doing what you've been doing. Make a conscious effort not to pull back with your body or with your words. Maintain a pleasant or moderately concerned expression and avoid nodding. Nodding can look like agreement on TV. Short answers to tough questions are fine, but don't make it sound as though you are giving a legal deposition.

Remember, too, an important point made in the last chapter: Don't respond to a tough question with a *non sequitur* or an obvious dodge. Acknowledge any elephants in the room. Owning up to your problems in a frank, sincere manner is the best way to boost credibility. The fastest way to do this is to focus on solutions.

I was working with the CEO of a fast-food chain when the issue of America's obesity problem was getting a lot of play. In a practice interview I asked whether this problem concerned him. He replied, "People are obese because they are inactive, not because of what they eat." I probed further—"*Isn't it a combination?*" But he wouldn't budge. He refused to acknowledge the link between food choice and weight issues. Worse, he *looked* miffed. Reporters are very good at picking up on sensitivities and would have zoned right in—Being a fierce competitor (like most top executives) this CEO would likely have become more entrenched. He was in a hole and would have kept digging. His was a losing battle and it would have eaten (pardon the pun) time he could have spent promoting the new salads his chain was developing as healthy menu choices. If he had done that, he and his company would have become part of the solution.

### *Never Mirror a Reporter's Mood*

One of the biggest style mistakes that people make is mirroring a reporter's personal style or mood. Take note: Reporters can use their style as a weapon.

When you are presenting, you must be hypersensitive to the mood of your audience, especially if audience members seem to be displaying any negative reaction. If you are speaking to, say, potential clients and you see confusion, skepticism or disagreement as you're talking, you must react. You should look and sound concerned. After all, you want to resolve all their issues and win them over to make a sale. With reporters you can almost always count on seeing skepticism and disagreement, but you rarely should react. They will often confront you with what your competition says about you or probe about the downside of your business model. Of course, they probably won't do this right away. In classic "interview sandwich" style, they may give you mixed signals—at first smiling, nodding, eliciting more positive information, then lowering the boom in mid-interview, then trying to wrap up in an affable fashion.

But if at any point a reporter displays negativity, keep your game face and plow ahead. This will dull the sword. Your intended audience—employees, customers, stakeholders—is most likely not going to notice an antagonistic reporter, but they will see you acting and looking like you're insecure or hostile. Even if you are under outright attack, even if you are feeling betrayed by a formerly friendly press member, assume a neutral demeanor and patiently explain the facts.

As a reporter I would use mood changes to lull someone suspected of wrongdoing into being very chatty and then use their words to connect to an apparent misdeed. In response, some heretofore calm and collected types would go ballistic, making it seem as though I'd definitely hit a nerve.

> **Me:** *I guess last month you and your board took a break from your tireless efforts and got some rest on the beach in Puerto Rico while your company went into Chapter 11.*
>
> **Interviewee:** *(sputtering and angry) Hey, how dare you accuse me? What do you mean by that? You have some nerve.*

Instead, he could have put the best possible face on what they'd done.

*Interviewee: (maintaining an even, congenial tone) Off-site meetings are common in the corporate world. We find people can brainstorm best free from daily pressures and constant interruptions. Let me tell you what we accomplished . . ."*

Your job as an interviewee is to be proactive, not reactive. Even if your angry reaction is justified, it won't go over well. This might not seem fair, but perception is reality.

## Controlling the Picture

If a reporter is coming to your turf and interviewing you in your office or at home, another important element of style involves controlling the picture. Look around and think about what you want your surroundings to say about you.

Settings are, of course, critical if your interview will be televised. But even if you are hosting a print reporter, your environment is important. A newspaper or magazine reporter might not get a shot of your surroundings, but rest assured the reporter will notice them and use the information to color the story. Reporters will be looking around for clues to your history, your pastimes, and your character.

### What's on Display?

When I was a reporter I would enter an office and quickly take in everything in one glance. Does this guy have a family? What sports does he like? What is his school affiliation, political affiliation?

If he has a wife in one picture, and is posing with three grown boys on a golf course in another, my opening line might be, "So you've got a ready-made foursome!" (I don't know a thing about golf beyond that, but that would loosen him up.) Now imagine that in another picture frame I see my interviewee at some extravagant corporate outing in a desert setting, wearing some kind of faux American Indian garb. He's on horseback, clicking cocktail glasses with a prominent senator. I may not use that as part of my opening greeting but it just might figure into my story somewhere down the line. Is his pharmaceutical company throwing extravagant shindigs and courting lawmakers? What are the voting records of those lawmakers on health and drug issues?

The point here is that the objects that are visible in your surroundings should send the signals you want to send. Displaying the fact that you're a solid family type is usually a positive, but if you've got some potentially embarrassing shots of yourself in a hula out-fit sharing umbrella drinks with members of an industry regulatory committee, consider putting them in temporary storage.

This isn't to suggest that you should make your office antiseptic, which in itself would suggest that you are hiding something, that you aren't really busy working, or that you have no "real life." I'm also not suggesting that you falsify your surroundings. (Golden retriever puppies are nice, but don't put a picture of one on your desk if your pet is a rottweiler.) Simply make it a practice to scan the room with a reporter's trained observant eye and put away anything that could be misinterpreted.

## Head over Heels

Choosing what's visible goes for documents, too. As a reporter I developed the skill of reading upside down. I learned a lot by looking at documents on people's desks as I awaited their arrival. A word to the wise . . .

### What's Your Context?

If you're going to be in a setting other than your office or living room, think what that setting suggests about you. A positive context can be invaluable as a message reinforcer.

A few years ago an executive for a large Midwestern chemical company was contacted by one of the big investigative television shows. The producer said they wanted to do a story on environmental impact. The executive and his public relations team felt they were in a good position and agreed to the interview. When the reporter and crew arrived, the PR person insisted they go out onto the lawn. It was a beautiful day—an *environmentally friendly* day. As it turned out, this was a great call. The reporter had some allegations about the company. The CEO defended the company's record well, and he looked great. Later, his own wife watched the story, only half listening to what he said (as is the way with married people sometimes). But her reaction was, "Honey you sounded fine and you looked wonderful out there in the great outdoors." The moral of the story is that a picture is worth a thousand words especially when people are not devoting their full attention.

On the other hand, even a positive message and honest answers can come off poorly when the context is incongruous. Take the case of a new dean of a business school who got cozy with a reporter and showed him not only the school's new classrooms but also his own lavish on-campus apartment. Now the dean used his apartment to entertain community leaders and attract speakers and wealthy alumni, but that isn't what people remembered. The reporter probably didn't want to undermine the dean, but he did want a good story. And his apartment no doubt made for a more interesting story, considering that tuition costs and academic perks have become so controversial.

### A Word on Wardrobe

In an earlier chapter I mentioned the importance of choosing your clothes carefully and not letting your clothes upstage you. Remember: nothing fashion forward, nothing tight or revealing, and—especially for television—no busy prints or tiny pinstripes. Even a print reporter might choose to write about your clothing, so be sure that the only thing that could be written about you is complimentary ("Looking the part of the relaxed, casual high-tech executive . . .").

Consistency is also a good idea. If you are doing multiple interviews, don't wear the same thing over and over (Steve Jobs in his black turtlenecks and Tom Wolfe in his white suits not withstanding), but do keep your overall look more or less the same. Keep your surroundings, the season, and the time of day in mind. (No tuxedos in the morning unless you won an Oscar and were up all night at the *Vanity Fair* party; no summer gear in winter unless you just rescued a baby whale marooned on an Australian reef.)

Above all, be comfortable in your clothes. If you are fidgeting because your collar is too tight it could come across as though you are fidgeting because you are not being truthful. People who look comfortable in their clothes seem comfortable in their own skin.

### Go to the Videotape

Before you do a press interview, I would urge you to videotape yourself delivering a presentation. From watching, you will see where you can improve your body language and demeanor. Watch for any peculiar mannerisms that you may want to curtail (maybe you didn't realize how often you straighten your eyeglasses or tug at your tie) and for things you do that seem to be especially effective (like making eye contact and smiling). Think about what might have worked in the presentation that might not work so well in an interview (maybe you need to modulate your voice a bit). Watch yourself through the eyes not only of a reporter but of your intended audience, and then serve your media message in the most flavorful way.

Makeup is also an issue especially for women. I am so glad high-definition television has arrived after my daily appearances. It is much less forgiving. Below is a list of makeup and grooming tips that I got from my former NBC makeup artist Patrick Denis.

### Mind Your Makeup: HDTV Tips for Looking Your Best

Eyes
- Pro shaped eyebrows—shade lighter than hair
- Natural matte eye shadow
- Black, brown or charcoal thin liner and mascara

Foundation and powder
- Yellow not pink undertone—match skin
- Sponge neck to cover red blotching
- Blush—tawny under cheekbones, not up to hairline and pinky/peachy under apple of cheek
- Powder—tinted and a shade lighter on face, under eyes, and neck

Lips and liner
- Medium tones—avoid blue or brown
- Some shine but not gooey

Men, you too! You may think that real men don't wear makeup but you really should in a TV studio. If nerves alone aren't enough, TV lights are harsh and can make you sweat. HDTV doesn't discriminate. It shows every little imperfection on men just like women. Most networks and major market TV stations employ makeup artists but they can get busy taking care of the big guns so I suggest BYOM—bring your own makeup. Head to the drug store and pick up foundation that is one shade darker than your skin. At the very least, buy some translucent powder that will even your skin tone and fight the shine.

## Top Tips

1. Use style to define your message more clearly and to indicate, "This is what I think is important."
2. Employ a natural and nondefensive style to dull the sword of negative questions and questioners.
3. Beware the interview sandwich—reporters tend to start and end affably; tough questions usually come in the middle.

# 18

# Making the Most of Your Moment

Throughout this book, I've talked about how important it is for speakers to be aware of time: how much has elapsed, how much do they have left, when do they need to cut it short and move things along? As this chapter will show, time sense is just as critical when you talk to the media as it is when you present. You need to learn to use your time wisely—to make the most of your moment, no matter how fleeting. And you need to budget your time differently for different types of media outlets.

## Tick Tock . . . Top Time Mistakes

Using your media time well can be tricky. When the clock is ticking it's all too easy to go off on a tangent that eats up precious moments, or to neglect to make the most of an unexpected opportunity. As a reporter and now, a communications coach, I've found that when it comes to time, the most common mistakes that interviewees make are:

Spending too much time on a subject that is off-topic or off-message. People who are high profile easily fall prey to spending too much time on one subject because they are opinionated and they think highly of their own opinions. However, they need to remember what they want to spend their time capital on.

For example, I was working with a celebrity who had lent his name to a charitable cause. As part of his preparation for a live interview, I asked him a political question: *Who was the best candidate for environmental issues?* and he went on and on, completely eating up the three minutes or so that would have been allotted to him. We played back the tape and he looked sheepish. He didn't get in a fraction of the information about the charity he wanted to plug, and he wasn't sure he wanted to commit to a politician anyway. Don't take bait like that, no matter how tempting!

What is even more common is experts spending too much time educating reporters instead of nailing a good quote, which should be the payoff for your time. I see this working with everyone from scientists to financial derivatives experts. The more complex their subject, the more likely they fall prey to the educator role. I remember a technology expert who spent an hour with a reporter only to see his information paraphrased and another expert quoted! Yes, it is important that the reporter have a good background, but this is not your main job. Part of your preparation should always be a little "lay of the land," basic information about what you do that anyone can understand. But if the reporter is really clueless you may need to e-mail him some background information or send him to a web site for basic information. And you may need to question whether you should be talking to this reporter at all.

**Spending too much time on a subject that is negative.** When a negative allegation is presented, people are often eager to go overboard about how they feel the allegation is unfair and why it holds no merit. Even if your defense sounds good, this isn't the type of content that you want quoted. Besides, if you go on for more than two sentences you are likely to open too many new doors. Stop while you're ahead or they'll have your behind!

**Spending too little time on your main message when you're given a green light.** When you catch the ball, run with it. If you get a question that's a great setup, give the reporter your best stuff. People often fear giving too long an answer to a juicy open-ended question, especially on live TV where there are strict time constraints. But let the reporter worry about stopping you—you just go for it.

For example, I was working with an author of a book about online dating. She was prepared to talk advice. But when a TV anchor first asked how she came up with her list of tips, she replied, "We asked our friends and family as well as dating web site clients." Then she stopped talking. The anchor looked a little surprised, expecting more, and scrambled to subjects that were related to online dating but didn't sell her book nearly as well. (Additionally, she was less likely to be invited back. Anchors don't like to have to pull answers out of people who are there to promote themselves.) In the future, the author ran with questions like that to explain what she'd actually asked her respondents: Is online dating more or less difficult now than five years ago? What was the thing that most surprised you? She learned to put meat on the bones and to speak freely when given the green light.

**Spending too much time on just one of your points.** If you are sitting dismayed at the end of your interview thinking, "Oh my gosh, they never asked me about such-and-such," then you were just the victim of bad time management, and *you* really are the one in charge of your time even when the media is involved.

In a business presentation with a client who only has 10 minutes, it's your job to say, "Bill, I'll be happy to send along additional information on trusts, but while I have you, I know you said you were also interested in philanthropy and hedge funds, so if it's all right with you I'll outline our services there and we can return to trusts when you have more time." If you do this with the right tone—one that makes it all about meeting their needs, everyone will be happy. So do the same thing with a reporter. If you don't ask, you don't get.

One of the reasons people make these mistakes where the press is concerned is that they don't understand the basics of how much time and space print and broadcast media allocate to their subjects. You've no doubt been reading newspapers and watching television for much of your life, but it's likely you've never really thought about this. Now it's time that you did!

## The Print Article: Size Matters

When a reporter calls you up and says he is doing a newspaper article, that could mean anything from a 300-word article (more typical of newspapers) to a 3,000 to 6,000-word piece (more common for a major magazine feature). In some cases the story might be all about you or your company, but in many cases you will be just a part of the story—one source among many.

In general, the amount of time devoted to your interview will depend on how important you are to the story. If you are one of several sources, you will probably be interviewed for 15 to 20 minutes. This is the most likely scenario. But if the reporter is just looking for a quote or a reaction, make that five minutes. In both cases, you will probably be interviewed by phone.

If you or what you are doing is the story, then you should allow an hour or more. In this case, the reporter will probably want to come to you and soak up the flavor of your surroundings (see the previous chapter on setting the stage so you will be sure to send the right signals). Figure 18.1 provides some general guidelines on how you should structure your communications time for both a 15-minute and 60-minute interview.

Naturally, part of being prepared is to find out what the focus of the story is, and how long, approximately, the interview will be

**PRINT**

- 15–20 minute interview so
  1 point per 5 to 7 minutes

- 60 minutes if you *are* the story

- 30 minutes maximum for your interview
  and the rest of the other executives,
  video footage of what you do.

**Figure 18.1   Print Time**

and how long the intended article will be. If you do this you can prepare your message modules accordingly. Because there is always the chance you will be cut short, get your best material in early.

Also, remember that with the convenience of e-mail, more and more reporters are willing to deliver a few questions in advance. See if you can get them to do so, as it will save both of you some time and ensure that you can deliver the goods.

Another courtesy you can request ahead of time is to have your quotes read back to you before they are printed. Ask nicely, because there is no obligation, but a reporter may comply if it's important to you. If they decline, you certainly have the right to decline the interview, but think about whether you really want to do so. Almost all interviewees are suspicious that their words may be taken out of context or edited in some other way that misrepresents them, but I think this is an overblown danger. Reporters almost always want to reflect your views accurately. Otherwise, they can't come back to you as a source. Besides, if they deliberately alter what you say, they could get in trouble with their publisher and even with the law.

### Too Many Cooks

Reporters don't like it when someone they are interviewing is surrounded by "handlers," especially when those handlers spend a lot of time saying, "He doesn't want to talk about this or that." It makes them suspicious there is something to hide. If there are negotiations to be done, it's best to get them taken care of before the interview takes place. Save the face time for *your* face.

## The TV Interview: "And Now for a Break . . ."

As with print interviews, the amount of time devoted to interviewing you for broadcast will depend on how integral you are to the story that is being covered. But with broadcast it will also depend on how much time the reporter has to pull everything together (not only interviews but visuals to support the story) and how important your story is relative to other stories in the newscast. In general, a pretaped interview will, like the average print interview, take 15 to 20 minutes. But only a fraction of that will air, especially if you're unlucky enough to be upstaged by a big breaking story, which could be anything from a major stock market dip to an earthquake, to the death, divorce, or arrest of a tabloid celebrity. Barring such unforeseen events, most pretaped news stories will be edited down to a minute and fifteen seconds or a minute and thirty seconds. If you are not the sole subject of the piece, your clips can be anywhere from five seconds to thirty seconds—a minute, tops, if you are a witness to breaking news ("And then the car just plowed into the front of the building. I couldn't believe my eyes"!)

If you are planning for a pretaped 15- to 20-minute interview, you should plan to use your best stuff right at the top. Use your headline to tell 'em what you're gonna tell 'em. Then, if you get the ball, run with it because a reporter in the editing room may have serious time constraints and use whatever comes up first that sounds good or even decent. Beyond that, be sure to cover all three of your message points. In a 15-minute interview you can elaborate on each point for approximately 5 minutes. Be sure to flag what is important; let the reporter know what you think. See Figure 18.2 for some guidelines on how to segment your speaking time for a taped segment.

**TAPED SEGMENT**

> 20 minute interview so
>
> > 1 point per  5 to 7 minutes
>
> - Give your best at the top
>
> - Flag what is important

**Figure 18.2    TV Time**

If you are doing a live interview, expect your segment to run for about three minutes. That's the perfect time in which to cover three message points. Allow for a 15- to 20-second setup by the reporter. Then allow one minute per point, which will usually consist of two questions and answers. If you see the reporter is not moving on from one topic, go ahead and bridge to the next thing you want to say.

Three minutes goes quickly, so be sure to rehearse putting your points into sound bites ahead of time.

For broadcast, try to talk in 10- to 15-second sound bites (about three typewritten lines). Get out a timer and time yourself to get comfortable with what that feels like. Figure 18.3 provides some insight into how to structure your time for live TV.

I worked with a retail financial analyst who was so adept at this she became my favorite sound-bite example. She always spoke in perfect four-line bites: "We see this as a crisis waiting to happen (headline module). For the last year such-and-such a company has been eliminating product lines while shoppers have passed them by (context). In fact, sales are down X% (fact module). We recommend investors pass them by, too; we've downgraded the stock to a sell" (summary module). At a young age she went on to found her own successful firm, and surely her skill with the media did not hurt.

**LIVE TV**

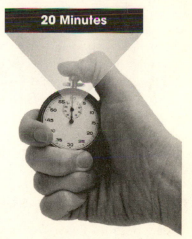

20 Minutes

3-minute segment

    1 point per minute or

2 (30 sec.) Q&A per point

- After answering second question move to next point

- 10–15 second anchor setup

- Run with the ball at the top

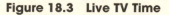

**Figure 18.3    Live TV Time**

## Preinterviews: Just as Important

If you are scheduled for a live interview, a producer will probably call you to conduct a preinterview. This will help ensure that your three minutes pack the most punch. Take those preinterviews seriously and prepare. Every interview with a reporter or producer counts. A pre-interview helps them decide how strong the story is.

I recently worked with a magazine reporter who had come up with a list of top web sites. A national network morning show spent an hour on a Saturday preparing her for a three-minute spot scheduled for Monday morning. There was nothing controversial in the interview, but the producer wanted to make sure the anchor would be armed with the best questions and that the interview guest would deliver interesting information. That is not to say the producer guided the guest to develop good quotes. That was up to her.

I know it can be unnerving to think about how fleeting a broadcast interview is. But, as always, a realistic view of what will happen, along with some good prep time on your part, will enable you to make the most of it. Besides, when it comes to interview time, you can actually have what I think is too *much* of it.

I was recently working with a top-drawer financial firm helping to prepare one of their executives for a big TV interview. The interview sounded like a good opportunity for the firm to show it was socially responsible. But like any financial firm, its primary *raison d'etre* was to do well for its investors. If the company could "do good" at the same time, great. So there were risks that the interview could go wrong. Because the firm's story was complex, its outside public relations firm advised that it extend the time for the interview to one full hour. I believe that is too long. A half hour is long enough to tell any story—more than that is enough time to take things off track. The lesson here: Be careful what you ask for; you just might get it.

## New Media: Is YouTube for You?

Today, people divide the time they devote to media among many more slices of the pie than they used to. They spend less time watching network evening newscasts, for example, but they may take that same amount of time—or more—and spend it browsing among several Internet sources for news. And that news might or might not come from reporters.

So, as important as it is to deal well with members of the press, it's important to keep in mind that traditional press coverage is not the only avenue available to you when you want to reach an intended audience of stakeholders, customers, and employees. YouTube videos, company web sites and personal blogs can all be used effectively to get messages out and to get them out with lightning speed. In fact, it is difficult to overemphasize the impact new media is having on the way people and organizations communicate.

New media messages can be used to instantly counter a negative public perception of a company. When Jet Blue Airways was receiving lots of bad press for canceling numerous flights in the aftermath of a storm, the company's CEO posted a video on YouTube, making a pledge to customers about how such situations would be handled in the future. Traditional media then covered *the video* as the story.

New media can also be used to keep concerned parties—including the press—updated during a crisis. Chrysler used its recently launched social media site to rapidly reach its employees, the media, and the public during a brief United Auto Workers strike. Ed Garsten, Chrysler's manager of communications, said of the site, "It's a tool that allows journalists and employees to quickly get information on the company and updates on the talks. And it allows the public to understand the issues that are involved."

But with opportunity also comes risk. The immediacy of new media can be a blessing, but there is also the temptation to put a message out there in cyberspace before you have really thought it through. Once you upload, there is simply no going back. If you've ever pressed "send" on an e-mail that you wrote in a huff and later regretted (and who hasn't?), you know what I mean.

The point is that when it comes to new media, you have to be just as thorough in your preparation as you would be when getting ready for an important presentation or press interview. Carefully consider who will be on the receiving end of the message. What do they want to know? Think about the content of your headline, your key points and all your message modules. Don't neglect to deliver your message with dignity and style (part of which is taking the time to cool off if you're in a snit).

Above all, don't wear out your welcome. Remember that Internet surfers have the shortest of short attention spans. According to Gary Brolsma of "Numa Numa" fame and voted "Greatest Internet Superstar" by VH1, "If you don't hook people in the first 15 seconds, they'll move on."

The legs and head of your communications tripod—audience, content, style, and time sense—are the same, whether you are dealing with old media or new. The difference between the two is that with new media, if you don't get it right, you can dig yourself a deeper hole at warp speed.

## Top Tips

1. Most interviews for print and taped broadcast run 15 to 20 minutes, but live broadcast interviews run about three minutes so plan your modules accordingly.
2. Get your best stuff out early—don't wait for them to ask.
3. Keep answers to negative or off-topic questions very short; don't squander your media moment.

# PART V

# A LAST WORD

# CHAPTER 19

# Oh No! Dealing with Worst-Case Scenarios

By now I hope I have thoroughly convinced you that the quintessential Boy Scout rule—*Be prepared!*—will provide you with peace of mind for your next communication event, whatever it may be. But in good conscience, I can't let you close this book without devoting this final chapter to those one-in-a-million occasions (well okay, they occur a *little* more often than that) when things go awry at the last minute.

Last-minute worst-case scenarios fall into three main categories: your equipment, your room, and the responses of people in the room. In this chapter we'll take a look at each in turn. The idea is that if you are aware of what can go wrong, you can lessen the impact. After all, a tornado can strike anytime, but those with a well-equipped cellar will be better off than their neighbors.

## Equipment: Tackling Technology Terrors

You gotta love good technology . . . except when it goes bad. When equipment fails, it can be horrid for you and your audience. Forget trying to exude the authority and credibility that are so important if you can't get your projector to project or your audio to be audible. And rest assured that when your videos freeze or your wireless clicker won't advance your slides, "A/V support" will be at lunch. Did I hear someone say, "Murphy's Law"?

When scenarios like these occur, the most important thing to remember is, *don't freeze when your technology does.* As a news anchor, I always had a hard copy of the news in front of me in case my teleprompter went down. I learned early the lesson I teach all my clients today: Anytime you are relying on technology, you must have a backup plan.

- Have hard copies of your slides printed and, if possible, ready to distribute so you can walk through them verbally.
- Have a backup copy on a CD/DVD, memory stick, or thumb drive to use on another computer.
- Be ready to move from high-tech to low-tech for visual support, for example using a flip chart or grease board as a PowerPoint substitute.
- Keep a little flashlight, extension cords, and a checklist for equipment (the latter is to make sure you are packing everything and can also repack quickly when the next conference room occupants are standing outside chomping at the bit).

Bottom line, as a presenter, you need to know your stuff—even if you didn't compose it—*and* be prepared to tap dance if you have to. Whatever you do, never whine or belabor the negative. It's perfectly all right to have a "bear with me" moment—trust me, everyone will empathize—but then you need to collect yourself. The show must go on, and when you can persevere you might earn bigger applause.

## When Technology Works and When It Shouldn't

Turn your PDA or your cell phone ringer off, and you might want to ask your audience to do so as well in a friendly "let's all focus for a few minutes" manner. I have mixed feelings about asking people to turn outside communication off entirely. If that is your preference, you can always point out that PDAs can interfere with PowerPoint projection, causing a deafening noise, a high price for others to pay for one guy not missing an e-mail.

As for you, I have actually seen people take calls while presenting. It is distracting to you and the audience, and it is just plain rude. It says you haven't prepared well. It says, "My time is more important than yours." Who knows if Rudy Giuliani meant to take a call from his wife on the stump, but it stumps me why he or anyone would.

### Avoiding Typo Trauma

Although you should double-check all the material on your slides, have someone other than you proof them. A third party is more likely to spot bloopers than is the original writer. But if a typo slips through don't apologize for it or highlight it in any way. Chances are no one will notice it unless *you* mention it.

## The Room: If Your Space Is a Disgrace

You don't always have control over picking the venue for your presentation and, as some of us know all too well, even a five-star hotel can have one dungeon-like conference room and you may be assigned to it. Still, it is your responsibility to make the best of what you've got and ensure that you and your audience will be as comfortable as possible.

If at all possible, get to the room in which you'll be presenting an hour before you are scheduled to go on. This will give you time to find out if everything you need is on hand or to come up with a "Plan B" if you can't get what you thought you'd have.

Be sure to check the room not only from your perspective but also from the perspective of your audience. Check the seating arrangements: Are there enough seats? Will everyone be able to see and take notes if they want? If note taking isn't needed, set up seating as indicated in Figure 19.1. See that chairs curve around you, the speaker. It is more inviting and feels more interactive than a classroom set up. Think theater in the round!

Take note of the acoustics and lighting in the room. Will people in the rear be able to see and hear? Do you need to wear a microphone and, if so, is it working? Will the sound in your video clips be audible to everyone? (If not, don't use them!) On the lighting front, don't douse them when you begin to show slides; just dim them so both you and your audience can see. (A totally darkened room provides too good a cover for a nap!) You'll also want to check for potential glare problems in the room.

**Distancing**

**Engaging**

**Figure 19.1    Smart Seating**

---

### Blowing Hot and Cold

If you have any control over the temperature in the room, exert that control. Remember that body heat increases room temperature so it will get warmer as more people enter. A room that's warm and toasty when you start out could be oppressive by the time you're midway through your talk. Again, good for napping—not listening.

---

## People Problems: You're Only Human . . . and So Is Your Audience

Whenever you are interacting with people, there will be unpredictable elements and your response to these problems will impact the response of your audience. No one can foresee every possible circumstance, but the following are scenarios that are not all that uncommon.

> **Your joke bombs:** While situational "organic" humor is always welcome, canned jokes can be lethal weapons. An executive experienced with business presentations on the international

stage warns his colleagues, "No joke is a good joke." He also reminds them, "Don't joke . . . and that's no joke." Jokes can fall flat at home and rarely if ever play well abroad. The same goes for cartoons. The British tend to appreciate slapstick (as any Monty Python devotee can attest) but a presenter who showed a slapstick-based cartoon to an Asian crowd found his audience was not only unamused, but also repelled. However, if you just can't help yourself and end up dropping a bomb, be prepared to smile, and move on. It happens to professional comedians all the time.

**You're thrown a hot potato:** Another unpredictable people problem is when you are suddenly thrust into the spotlight. The same executive told me about a boss who, seeing he had 10 minutes to fill while the next speaker figured out his technology problems, tossed the ball to *him*! Yes, he asked him to improvise in front of 500 people. That is when he learned how handy it is to have a filler module! The company this executive works for happens to make a popular line of snacks (let's call them Yummy Yums) that have been subject to increasing competition, so he stood up and polled the audience: How many of you grew up with "Yummy Yums?" (Show of hands.) How many of you have them in your cabinet today? He filled time and made a point: Yummy Yums are under pressure but they still sell a lot and they still have emotional resonance.

**You have a wardrobe malfunction:** Corporate wardrobe malfunctions rarely rise to the Janet Jackson level. But haven't all of us spilled something on a white garment, or noticed in the light of day (after dressing in dim light so as not to wake our spouse) that our socks, our shoes, or even the two halves of our suits don't match? If you're getting ready to pitch for that opportunity of a lifetime even a little errant jelly from a doughnut can make you want to crawl into a cave and die. You can quickly lose all the confidence you've been building. Well, *stop that*. People probably won't notice, and even if they do, they care more about what you have to say. If anyone deigns to point out your stain or your mismatch, go for empathy. Say: *Don't you just hate when that happens!* And move on.

**You lose your place and your thought flow, coming up empty:**
Here I always think of Jeanne Piro, a former district attorney,
when she ran against Hillary Clinton for a New York Senate
seat. Just as she was lambasting her opponent she turned
the page and, well . . . the page was missing. Watching her
go silent for what seemed an interminable pause reminded
me of a dream I still have every few years where I'm sitting
at an anchor desk for an update without a script and the red
light goes on—*talk*, Mary!—but I have nothing. However,
Piro did something worse than freezing. She snapped at her
staff, "*Where* is page eleven?" Her first misstep was not knowing her own material well enough to wing it: What *did* she
think about Hillary's performance? Her second mistake was
failing to realize that most of the people watching, potential
voters, related to her staffers more than to the well-dressed
lawyer behind the podium—and they wouldn't want to be
snapped at. This politician had seriously damaged her likeability and leadership quotient.

We all lose our place sometimes, even if we don't actually
misplace a page of type. It's a good opportunity to exhibit
humor and grace under pressure. Piro should have said,
"I don't have the next page of my remarks here," (signaling
her need to her team) but then continued with the gist of
what she wanted to say. It would probably have been more
heartfelt than what was written down, anyway.

**You make a poor choice of words and put your foot in your
mouth:** Don't call attention to small gaffes; just move on.
But if you have made an obvious and serious blunder, apologize and *then* move on. If you have offended one person in
particular, approach that individual later and elaborate. This
happened to me once. I was coaching presentations and in
one practice presentation a gentleman referred to a relative
who had died. It was part of a very long story and the death
wasn't clear, at least to me. In fact, the way I heard it was
that it was a *brush* with death that had moved him to take a
job with this particular charity. I summarized his presentation incorrectly and asked about the health of his relative
today. I hurt him and myself. The miscommunication indicated either that his presentation was flawed or that I wasn't
listening. I apologized.

## Generation Gap?

Ours is a multigenerational workplace. And sometimes we're surprised to find ourselves talking with a group of people who are significantly older or younger. This can create some communication gaps, so keep the following guidelines in mind.

If you are young (south of 40) talking to older colleagues:

- Watch singsong delivery, where inflection goes up at the end of a sentence as if asking a question. "So, we looked at all the *data*?"
- Forget "like." The 40-plus crowd doesn't like "like." Like, I know you've heard this before but, like it really irks your older colleagues so, like why create friction when you don't have to?

If you are older (north of 40) talking to younger colleagues:

- Watch the stories about yesteryear: "I walked uphill to school, both ways." It usually celebrates you and your generation rather than connecting to your audience. (A colleague of mine, Jim Gray, surveyed young people and this came through on the top of their list of pet peeves.)
- Act your age. Don't try to talk cool or "ku-ehl" or say you're "down with it" unless you're intent on appearing downright pitiable.

Interactivity is especially important for anyone addressing a different generation. Younger people should mine the minds of the older crowd. They'll gain respect by doing so, and learn things only experience can teach. Older people should pick the brains of younger people. It will build relationships and enhance understanding of the customers of tomorrow. Besides, you never know if a younger person will end up being your boss.

**You are late . . . very late:** Stuff happens. No matter how much you prize punctuality you can run into unforeseen speed bumps. It happened to me. I was en route to see top executives at a major client in Manhattan when I remembered that I had forgotten an important document. I took a miscalculated risk and went back to get it. Hey, it was the middle of the day, not rush hour—but President Bush had come to town and traffic was seriously backed up. When I finally arrived at the meeting, everyone had those raised-eyebrow "so glad you could make it" looks on their faces. While I was tempted to share my myriad mishaps, I practiced what I preach for such circumstances: Apologize sincerely but briefly. No one *cares* what your excuse is, legitimate or contrived. You have kept people waiting so don't multiply the problem. Get on with it and *be good*.

---

### Top Tips

1. Whatever goes wrong, don't dwell on it—don't belabor the negative.
2. Have backup materials at the ready for when primary technology fails.
3. Keep your sense of humor!

---

## Final Thoughts . . .

I sincerely hope you never find yourself in an awkward communications scenario. But if you present often enough, if you try new things, you will make a few mistakes. Those are the odds. (Just as if you drive every day you will probably get a ticket at one time or another.) But, if you don't take risks, you risk not becoming the most persuasive and dynamic speaker you can be. You know, as I write this, there have been a few articles written that actually seem to deemphasize the importance of good communication.

Ushering in a new year, Carol Hymowitz at the *Wall Street Journal* said last year was all about spin. This year, in a tougher economy, she predicted business people will be graded more heavily on strategy.

But spin alone has never been good communication. There has to be meat between the buns. And, no matter how strong your strategy, you won't be able to sell it internally or externally without clear communication. Communication counts in every business, in every endeavor, and in any economy.

So take the time to practice. Don't try too much too fast. Try new things when the stakes aren't high. If, for example, you have never tried walking when presenting, try it out in front of your direct reports or colleagues who will support your effort, even if they tell you to scrap the plan.

Finally, never forget:

*Audience:* Remember to interpret why what *you* propose will be of value to *them*.

*Substance:* Remember the power of just three key points.

*Style:* Remember to move the needle by what you say and do, and move your modules to keep things fresh.

*Time:* Remember no one has enough of it, so use this precious resource wisely.

Should missteps occur, stay calm, keep smiling, and remember that such things can, and do, happen to the best of us. Try to see the lighter side. Keep in mind that today's awful mishap is tomorrow's hilarious anecdote. As all good storytellers know, everything is grist for the mill.

Besides, whatever goes wrong, much more will go right if you hold on to all you've learned. Keep reminding yourself how much communication counts. Equip yourself with strong modules, get to know them well enough that you can move them around and regularly hit that refresh button. Approach the process with thoroughness, logic, a good attitude, and a profound respect for those who will be listening to you. If you do this, you will begin to count your victories.

# About the Authors

**Mary Civiello** is president of Civiello Communications Group, a presentation and media consultancy. A former television reporter and anchor for NBC in New York as well as CNBC and MSNBC, Mary has earned accolades on both sides of the microphone. Over her 20 years in TV news she won six Emmys and the prestigious Sigma Delta Chi Deadline Club award. As a coach she was dubbed the corporate executive's "Communication Guru" by the *New York Times*.

Mary's clients include top executives at many of the Fortune 100 companies. She also coaches non-profit groups, celebrity spokespeople and politicians on both sides of the aisle. In addition to providing communications advice, Mary is a regular commentator in the media discussing communication style and effectiveness.

For more information on Mary and Civiello Communications Group, or to download worksheets referred to in this book, please visit www.civiello.com.

**Arlene Matthews** is the author and co-author of numerous books on the topics of business communications, stress management, popular psychology, and parenting. Her work has also been published in numerous magazines and newspapers, including *Money* magazine, *Poets & Writers*, the *San Francisco Chronicle*, and the *Washington Examiner*.

# Index

## A

Accenture, 126

Adjusting length of modules, 95–98

Ad line, using as signpost, 125

Advancing slides, 136

Advertising, and headline module, 57–58

"Aha!" statement, finding, 55–57

Aisenbrey, Chris, 40

Alsop, Ronald, 40

Ambush, handling, 187–189

Analogies:
  classifying and filing, 23, 24
  coming up with, 126
  proofs module and, 17–18

Anecdotes:
  coming up with, 61, 127–128
  proofs module and, 18
  worn, 117–118

Anxiety about public speaking, reframing, 27

Aristotle, 42

Attention:
  of Internet surfers, 210
  recapturing during presentation, 5

Attention span, length of, 4, 88–89

Attitudes:
  communicating about, 68
  interactivity and, 137–138

Audience:
  asking to turn off electronics, 214–215
  body language of, 94
  captive, myth of, 6
  connecting with, 40–41, 133–134
  dressing like best in, 141–142
  due diligence for, 46–47
  as essential element of communication, 10
  fine-tuning presentation for, 39
  interactivity and, 137–138, 219
  international, 161–165
  at meetings, 117–118
  message tripod and, 12–13
  of one, presenting to, 48–49
  for panel presentation, 158
  problems with, 216–220
  Q&A session, handling during, 147–149
  quieting, 69–70, 118

Audience *(continued)*
   reacting to video with, 139
   reporters and, 169–170
   respecting, 44–46
   WIIFM (What's In It for Me?)
     and, 41–44
Audience slip off, 89
Author, web site of, 84
Axtell, Roger, *Gestures: The Do's
   and Taboos of Body Language
   Around the World,* 162

**B**

"Baby signing," 76
Back pocket module, 116–117
Backup plan for technology
   problems, 213–215
Bartiromo, Maria, 174, 186
Bashing press, 176
Believability, fear of not
   demonstrating, 30
Berger, Dennis, 57–58
Bernanke, Ben, 174
Biography, and context
   module, 17
Blacking out slides, 134
Blair, Tony, 71
Blank, drawing, 31–33, 218
Blogosphere, 174
Body language:
   of audience, 94
   reading, 110
   of speaker, 69
Boilerplate speech:
   description of, 15
   one-minute message, 104–106
Boss, presenting to, 48–49
Boundaries, respecting,
   108–110

Boycotts of words, 83
BP, 30–31
Brain, training to think in
   modules, 20–24
Breathing, importance of, 36
Bridging to message, 185–187
Broadcast interview:
   live, 207–208
   taped, 205–206
   *See also* Media interview
Brolsma, Gary, 210
Buffett, Warren, 81
Bull, killing, 29
Business, pitching to decision
   makers, 43–44
Business casual dress, 142
Business schools, 40–41

**C**

Calling on someone in
   audience, 94
Call to action module:
   description of, 19
   headline module and, 62
   international audience
     and, 164
   in one-minute message, 106
   pacing and, 79
   time for, 95
Captive audience, myth of, 6
Castro, Fidel, 88
Cell phone call during meeting,
   214–215
Cerf, Vint, 132
Challenger, disarming, 115–116
Checking facts, 125–126
Chertoff, Michael, 147
Chrysler, 209
Churchill, Winston, 35

Classifying message modules,
  21–24
Clinton, Bill, 77, 78
Clinton, Hillary, 124, 147, 218
Clothing, 141–142, 198, 217
Cochran, Johnnie, 19
Cognitive aspect of fear, 28–33
Colorful quotes, 182
Common ground, finding, 185
Conference calls, 155
Confronter, handling, 148
Connecting with audience,
  40–41, 133–134
Consultation with doctor, 91
Content:
  creating new, 21
  matching tone to, 80–81
  slides as leading, 133
Context, environmental,
  choosing for interview,
  197–198
Context module:
  creating, 123–124
  description of, 17
  headline module and, 62
  for media interview, 181–182
  time for, 95
Controversial information,
  delivering, 81
Conversational tone:
  of media message, 194
  of one-minute message,
  106–108
Cool rule, 83–84
Crawl, The, 6–7
Credibility:
  delivering controversial
  information and, 81
  fear of not demonstrating,
  30–31

simplicity and, 52–53
standing and, 114
Culture, familiarity with,
  162–165, 217
Cut to the chase, 89–91

**D**

Data-laden slides, 134
Decision style, matching
  presentation to, 48–49
Deep breathing, 36
DeGaulle, Charles, 185
Delivery style for media
  message, 192–196
Denis, Patrick, 199
Disarming challenger, 115–116
Disrupter, handling, 149
Doctor, consultation with, 91
Documents, covering, 197
"Do what you love" speech of
  Jobs, 19–20, 73
Drawing blank, 31–33, 218
Dress, style of, 141–142, 198, 217
Dressing up message, 57–58
Due diligence for audience,
  46–47

**E**

Ebbinghaus, Hermann, 4, 5, 8
Editing speech at last minute,
  31–33
Educator role, 202
Electronics, asking audience to
  turn off, 214–215
Elevator speech (one-minute
  message), 104–106
Emotion:
  communicating about, 68
  memory and, 8

Emotional quotes, 182, 183
Empty, coming up, 31–33, 218
Energy, projecting, 192
Entrance, making, 69–70
Essential elements of speaking,
    8–11
Euphemisms, 83
Everett, William, 87
Exaggeration, and credibility,
    30–31
Experimenting with message
    modules, 24
Eye contact, 72–74, 136

**F**

The Face: A Natural History
    (McNeill), 70
Facts:
    classifying and filing, 23, 24
    finding and checking,
        125–126
    proofs module and, 17
Factual quotes, 182–183
Fairness appeal, 148
Fear busters, 33–34
Fear of public speaking:
    cognitive aspect of, 28–33
    overview of, 25
    physical aspect of, 26–27
Fear of vulnerability, 54–55
Fifth grade level, gearing
    message toward, 29
Fight or flight response, 26–27
First, speaking, 119
First impressions, 110–111
Fitzwater, Marlin, 146
Five-minute meeting modules:
    audience for, 117–118
    back pocket, 116–117

    disarming challengers, 115–
        116
    formula for, 113–114
    style and, 118–119
Flip chart, using, 122–123, 139
Focus change, 32–33
Forgetting curve, 4, 7–8
Freshening headline, 64–65

**G**

Gandhi, Mahatma, 25
Gaps, noticing, 21
Garsten, Ed, 209
Gates, Bill, 81
Generational issues, 219
Gestures, 75–77, 192
Gestures: The Do's and Taboos of
    Body Language Around the
    World (Axtell), 162
Gettysburg Address, 87
Giuliani, Rudy, 215
Goldin-Meadow, Susan, 76
Gore, Al, An Inconvenient
    Truth, 132
Graph, message conveyed by,
    134–135
Gray, Jim, 219

**H**

Hallin, Daniel, We Keep
    America on Top of the
    World, 88–89
Handlers, 205
Hands behind back, placing, 76
Hayes, Helen, 27
HDTV, 199
Headline module:
    delivering, 51

description of, 16
fear of vulnerability and, 54–55
finding and writing, 55–58
freshening, 64–65
generating, example of, 62–64
language of, 58–60
linking to other modules, 60–62
for media interview, 180–181
oversimplifying and, 52–53
time sense and, 89–90, 95
History:
  of company, beginning with, 53–54
  of speaking, remembering, 34–35
Homer, 131
Homework, doing before speaking to reporter, 175
Humor:
  anecdotes and, 128
  culture and, 162
  jokes and, 216–217
Hymowitz, Carol, 220
Hyperbole, 59

**I**

Importance, recognizing, 53
Improvise, being asked to, 217
*An Inconvenient Truth* (movie), 132
Incorporating questions into presentation, 144–145
Insider terms, 59
Intelligent, appearing, and fear of public speaking, 28–29

Interactivity, 137–138, 219
International audience, presenting to, 161–165
International Listening Association, 41
Interview, appealing to audience at, 40, 42–43. *See also* Media interview
"Interview sandwich" style, 195
Introducing product, 141
Inventory, taking, 21

**J**

Jargon, steering clear of, 107–108, 193–194
Jerry Springer show, 178
Jet Blue Airways, 209
Jobs, Steve, "do what you love" speech of, 19–20, 73
Jokes, telling, 128, 216–217
Jolt so they won't bolt:
  listening curve and, 5
  strategies for, 92–94

**K**

Kerry, John, 77
Kissinger, Henry, 185

**L**

Language:
  culture and, 163–164
  jargon, 107–108, 193–194
  overly complex, 58
Laser pointer, 136–137
Late, arriving, 219–220
Leader, designating for team presentation, 152
"Legs," stories with, 56

Length:
   of attention span, 4, 88–89
   of long speech, streamlining,
      129
   of main attraction modules,
      121
   of modules, adjusting, 95–98
Lighting, 215
Likeability:
   fear of not demonstrating, 31
   smiling and, 70–71
Lincoln, Abraham, and
      Gettysburg Address, 87
Linking headline module to
      other modules, 60–62
Listening curve, 5
Live interview, 207–208
Lockstep rhetoric, 82–83
Lowering voice, 78
Lyons, Janet, 58

**M**

Main attraction modules:
   context module for, 123–124
   creating in order, 123
   format for, 122–123
   length of, 121
   proofs module for, 125–128
   rehearsing, 128–129
   signpost module for, 124–125
Makeup, 199
Marking up speech, 73, 129
Matching tone to content,
      80–81
M.B.A. student recruiting
      process, 40
McGovern, George, 26
McNeill, Daniel, *The Face:*
      *A Natural History,* 70

Media interview:
   ambush, handling, 187–189
   environment for, 196–199
   formula for, 206, 207
   hardball questions, 184–187
   live, 207–208
   modules for, 179–183
   preinterview, 208
   preparing for, 177–178
   for print article, 204–205
   return on investment of time
      and effort for, 179
   softball questions, 183–184
   taped, 205–206
   time sense and, 201–203
   *See also* Reporter
Media message:
   delivery style for, 192–196
   for new media, 208–210
   serving with spice, 191–192
Meeting modules:
   audience for, 117–118
   back pocket, 116–117
   disarming challengers,
      115–116
   five-minute, formula for,
      113–114
   style and, 118–119
Mehrabian, Albert, 68, 82
Memory:
   decline of, in forgetting
      curve, 4
   retention rate, increasing,
      7–8
   short-term, challenges of, 3–4
   stress and, 5–6
Message modules:
   case study of, 19–20
   categories of, 16–19
   description of, 15

editing at last minute and,
31–33
for media interview, 179–183
one-minute, 103–101
for team presentation,
152–153
timing and adjusting, 95–98
training brain to think in,
20–24
*See also* Main attraction
modules; Media message;
Meeting modules
Message tripod, 12–13
Middle of presentation, 92–94
Mind crawl, 7
Mirroring mood or personal
style, 195–196
Misunderstanding, correcting,
185
Moderating panel presentation,
156–157
Modular communication
strategies, xiii–xv. *See also*
Message modules; *specific
modules*
Mood:
mirroring, 195–196
shifting, 72
Movement:
gestures, 75–77, 192
natural, 74–75
Mozart, 136

**N**

Neutral tone of voice, 81, 195
New media message, 208–210
Newscast, 92–93
Newspaper article, 204–205
News story, length of, 88–89

Nitpicker, handling, 149
Nodding, 194
Noonan, Peggy, 26
Notes, reading from, 192–193
Numbers, padding headlines
with, 60

**O**

Obama, Barack, 124
Office, environment of,
196–197
One-minute message:
boilerplate for, 104–106
conversational tone of,
106–108
first impressions and,
110–111
opportunities for, 108–110
overview of, 103–104
Open and close effect, 4
Opening presentation, 89–91
O'Reilly, Bill, 179
Organizing message modules,
21–24
Overselling, 30–31
Oversimplifying, 52–53
Overtime, going, 98–99

**P**

Pacing, 78–79
Panel presentation:
description of, 151, 156
moderating, 156–157
participating in, 157–159
Past:
context module and, 17
history of company,
beginning with, 53–54
Pause, employing, 79, 193

Persuasion:
   pitch and, 80
   standing and, 114
Physical aspect of fear, 26–27
Physical presentation model,
      74–75
Picture, message conveyed by,
      134–135
Piro, Jeanne, 218
Pitch of voice, 79–81
Place, losing, 218
Planting question, 147
Podium, walking away from,
      74–75
Pointing verbally, 29
Points module, 17
Powell, Colin, 140
PowerPoint:
   interactivity and, 137–138
   slide content, 133–136
   uses of, 132–133
"PowerPoint Is Evil" (Tufte), 132
Preinterview, 208
Preparing:
   for media interview, 177–178
   for question-and-answer
      session, 144
   videotaping presentation, 67,
      68, 129, 198–199
   See also Rehearsing
Presentation evaluation
      form, 84
Press bashing, 176
Previewing slides, 136
Print article, 204–205
Product, introducing, 141
Projecting energy, 192
Proofing material, 215
Proofs module:
   believability and, 30

creating, 125–128
description of, 17–18
for media interview,
      182–183
Props, power of, 140–141
Public relations (PR) team, 178
Public speaking, fear of:
   cognitive aspect of, 28–33
   overview of, 25
   physical aspect of, 26–27
Putting foot in mouth, 218

**Q**

Question-and-answer (Q&A)
      session:
   being proactive and
      controlling, 145–147
   handling difficult audience
      members during,
      147–149
   international audience
      and, 165
   overview of, 143
   preparing, 144
   silence as response to,
      149–150
Questions:
   ambush, handling, 187–189
   asking, 93, 144–145, 149–150
   media question control,
      183–187
   planting, 147
   reframing, 185
   from reporter, getting in
      advance, 205
   solutions, focusing on when
      answering, 194
Quid pro quo, 186
Quieting audience, 69–70, 118

Quote:
    having reporter read back, 205
    memorable, 182–183, 202

**R**

Reacting to video with
    audience, 139
Reading:
    PowerPoint slides
        verbatim, 136
    from prepared notes, 192–193
Reagan, Ronald, 26
Rebound technique, 145
Recruiting M.B.A. students, 40
Reed, John, 186
Reframing:
    anxiety about public
        speaking, 27
    questions, 185
Regulation Fair Disclosure, 155
Rehearsing:
    gestures, 77
    jolts, 94
    long presentations, 128–129
    media interviews, 198–199
    movements, 75
    presentations, 68
    projecting energy, 192
    team presentations, 153
    See also Preparing
Relationship between speaker
    and listener, 41–42
Reporter:
    audaciousness of, 172–173
    audience and, 169–170
    curiosity and suspiciousness
        of, 171–172
    as generalist, 174–175
    as getting people
        comfortable, 173
    informality of, 173
    mirroring mood or personal
        style of, 195–196
    questions from, getting in
        advance, 205
    researching, 175
    slipperiness of, 174
    speaking to, 169
    understanding, 170–171
Researching reporter, 175
Respecting:
    audience, 44–46
    social boundaries, 108–110
Retention rate, increasing, 7–8
Reverse analogy, 126
Rhetoric, lockstep, 82–83
Ricochet technique, 145
Risk-averse type, presenting
    to, 49
Risks, taking, 220
Risk taker, presenting to, 48
Room, problems with, 215–216
Russert, Tim, 140

**S**

Seating arrangement, 215, 216
Shortened presentation time,
    handling, 96–98
Short-term memory, challenges
    of, 3–4
Signpost module:
    classifying and filing, 21–22
    creating, 124–125
    description of, 19
    headline module and, 62
Simplicity and credibility, 52–53
Situation, reading, 110
Size of gestures, 77
Skeptical type, presenting to, 49
Slang, 83–84

Slides:
    content of, 133–136
    proofing, 215
    time on screen, 8
Smiling, 70–72, 192
Social boundaries, respecting,
    108–110
Social media site, 209
Solutions, focusing on, 194
Sound bite, length of, 88–89
Space for presentation,
    problems with, 215–216
Speaking first at meeting, 119
Speech rate, 8
Stage fright:
    cognitive aspect of, 28–33
    overview of, 25
    physical aspect of, 26–27
Standing to deliver update, 114
Storytelling formula, 127–128
Streamlining long speech, 129
Strengths, playing to, 153
Stress:
    fight or flight response and,
        26–27
    memory and, 5–6
Stump speech, 15
Style:
    as essential element of
      communication, 10
    media messages and, 192–196
    meeting modules and, 118–119
    message tripod and, 12–13
    substance and, 67–68
    team presentation and,
        154–155
    variety and, 84
    verbal elements of, 82–84
    visual elements of, 69–77
    vocal elements of, 77–81

Substance:
    as essential element of
      communication, 10
    message tripod and, 12–13
    style and, 67–68
    *See also* Headline module
Summarizing message, 16, 19
Summary module:
    description of, 19
    for media interview, 183
    pacing and, 79
    time for, 95

**T**

Talker, dealing with, 69–70, 118
Team presentation:
    description of, 151
    number of members for, 154
    planning for, 151–154
    style and, 154–155
Teaser test, 57
Technology, problems with,
    213–215
Television interview, *see* Media
    interview
Television techniques,
    translating to real world, xii
Temperature of room, 216
Thoughtful type, presenting
    to, 49
Three points to reinforce
    headline, 60
Threes, power of, 17, 18, 60
3 × 3 formula, 60–62
Time sense:
    culture and, 164
    cut to the chase, 89–91
    definition of, 88
    developing, 88–89

as essential element of
communication, 10–11
Gettysburg Address and, 87
going over time allotment,
98–99
jolt so they don't bolt, 92–94
media interview and, 201–203
message tripod and, 13
modules, timing and
adjusting, 95–98
Tone of voice:
conversational, 106–108, 194
matching to content, 80–81
neutral, 81, 195
pitch and, 79–81
Training brain to think in
modules, 20–24
Transitions, 29
Tufte, Edward, "PowerPoint Is
Evil," 132
Twain, Mark, 104
Twenty-minute message
modules:
context module for, 123–124
creating in order, 123
format for, 122–123
overview of, 121
proofs module for, 125–128
rehearsing, 128–129
signpost module for, 124–125

**U**

U.S. Congress, one-minute
speeches of, 108

**V**

Variety, 84
Verbal elements, 82–84
Verbal gaffe, 218

Video:
environment for, 196–199
using, 138–139
Videotaping presentation, 67,
68, 129, 198–199
Visual elements:
body language, 69
entrance, making, 69–70
eye contact, 72–74
flip chart, 139
gestures, 75–77, 192
laser pointers, 136–137
natural movement, 74–75
power of, 131
presenter as, 141–142
props, 140–141
as road to interactivity,
137–138
smiling, 70–72, 192
video, 138–139
*See also* PowerPoint
Vocal elements:
overview of, 77–78
pacing, 78–79
tone and pitch, 79–81
volume, 78
*See also* Tone of voice
Volume, 78
Vulnerability, fear of, 54–55

**W**

Walking away from podium,
74–75
Wardrobe, 141–142, 198, 217
Web site of author, 84
*We Keep America on Top of the
World* (Hallin), 88–89
What's In It for Me? (WIIFM),
41–44

Whirlpool Corporation, 40
Words:
   boycotts of, 83
   poor choice of, 218
Work-related functions, 111
Worst-case scenarios:
   handling, 221
   people problems, 216–220
   space is disgrace, 215–216

technology, problems with,
   213–215
Writing:
   headline, 55–58
   presentation, 35

**Y**

YouTube, 209